"This anthology stands out as a constellation of inspired lights. They shine as guiding stars toward the rejuvenation of our souls, and a necessary resource to grow our sanctified imagination." —MAKOTO FUJIMURA, artist, author of *Art+Faith: A Theology of Making*

"For one who has steeped himself in theology for decades, it's a pleasure to discover poems imbued with the truth, goodness, and beauty of the Christian faith." —MARK GALLI, former editor in chief of *Christianity Today,* and publisher of *Peripheral Vision*

"All poets can see that *in the beginning was the Word.* They might even discern that *the Word was God.* But how do they perceive that *the Word was made flesh, and dwelt among us?* For that last step, the addition of faith, makes all the difference. The poets gathered here have all made the leap of faith—and it thickens their verse into one of the best anthologies in decades." —JOSEPH BOTTUM, Poetry editor, *New York Sun*

"The most comprehensive anthology of modern Christian poetry I have seen, including notable voices from across the various denominations of the Church. If Christians are to know the poetic voice of God, they would do well to train their ears with the verses of these disciples." —JESSICA HOOTEN WILSON, author of *The Scandal of Holiness*

"The works and writers assembled here provide just the right mix and quality of technical sharpness, intellectual acuity, and spiritual food that this age of cheap pleasures and lost eloquence needs so much. It's a trove of expression for the mind and the soul." —MARK BAUERLEIN, editor at *First Thing*

"This volume gives the lie to those who complain that believers in Christ have abandoned the fine arts. There are still many poets out there with their sleeves rolled up, ready to wrestle with temporal and eternal issues." —LOUIS MARKOS, Professor in English and Scholar in Residence, Houston Baptist University; author of *The Myth Made Fact: Reading Greek and Roman Mythology through Christian Eyes*

"Keep this book somewhere you can easily find it, because you'll want to return to it again and again. The poems here will linger with you, and so will the wisdom on how to read them. You won't see the words 'Christian poetry' the same ever again." —RUSSELL MOORE, Chair of Theology, *Christianity Today*

"In the distinctively American chapel erected by *Christian Poetry in America*, brief yet perceptive introductions to each poet frame the selections and orient readers to the many facets of Christian practice and poetic art that form this living tradition. By inviting us to step inside America's vibrant chapel of Christian poetry, Mattix and Thomas have given the church a rich gift." —JEFFREY BILBRO, Associate Professor of English at Grove City College and editor-in-chief at *Front Porch Republic*

"I am often asked to recommend poets and poetry collections to readers who don't know where to begin. I am delighted to have this volume now, one I will recommend again and again." —KAREN SWALLOW PRIOR, Research Professor of English and Christianity & Culture at Southeastern Baptist Theological Seminary, author of *On Reading Well: Finding the Good Life through Great Books*

"Judicious in their selections and richly informative both in their introduction to the volume and introductions to each poet, [Mattix and Thomas] have given lovers of fine poetry a treasure trove of good reading and a welcome textbook for college classrooms." —DAVID LYLE JEFFREY, author of *Translations: A Collection of Poems* and *Scripture and the English Poetic Imagination*

"Good poetry is the distillation of language into its purest form. This is especially true of good Christian verse which is the distillation of mere words into purest spirit. This new anthology is a great blessing, offering a joyful spiritual retreat into the presence of the beauty of words and into the presence of the beauty of the Word Himself." — JOSEPH PEARCE, The Augustine Institute, editor of *Poems Every Catholic Should Know*

"If the question is whether the poets in this anthology have a claim on serious readers of poetry, the answer is an engaging yes. One soon finds that these writers are more committed to art than they are possessed by politics. Their beliefs compel them to think as individuals. In their moral seriousness, they tap wellsprings of emotion that may prove to be vitalizing for American literature." —LEE OSER, College of the Holy Cross

"Broadly representative and inclusive: there is room here for Roman Catholics and Episcopalians, Baptists and Mennonites, for doubting Thomases and repenting Peters and irritated Jeremiahs, for those whom hope eludes as well as for those whom joy surprises. And there is room for both formalism and open form poems, for tradition and experiment. I'll be recommending the collection to my colleagues and students." —WILLIAM TATE, Covenant College

CHRISTIAN POETRY IN AMERICA

SINCE 1940: AN ANTHOLOGY

EDITED BY

Micah Mattix and Sally Thomas

IRON
PEN

PARACLETE PRESS
BREWSTER, MASSACHUSETTS

2022 First Printing

Christian Poetry In America Since 1940: An Anthology

Copyright © 2022 by Paraclete Press, Inc.

Trade Paper ISBN 978-1-64060-723-1
Hardcover ISBN 978-1-64060-812-2

The Iron Pen name and logo are trademarks of Paraclete Press.

   Library of Congress Cataloging-in-Publication Data
Names: Mattix, Micah, 1972- editor. | Thomas, Sally, 1964- editor.
Title: Christian poetry in America since 1940 : an anthology / edited by
   Micah Mattix and Sally Thomas.
Description: Brewster, Massachusetts : Iron Pen/Paraclete Press, [2022] |
   Summary: "A compilation of important Christian poetry of the last eighty
   years"-- Provided by publisher.
Identifiers: LCCN 2022011382 (print) | LCCN 2022011383 (ebook) | ISBN
   9781640608122 (hardcover) | ISBN 9781640607231 (paperback) | ISBN
   9781640607248 (epub) | ISBN 9781640607255 (pdf)
Subjects: LCSH: Christian poetry, American. | American poetry--20th
   century. | American poetry--21st century.
Classification: LCC PS595.C47 C47 2022 (print) | LCC PS595.C47 (ebook) |
   DDC 811/.5408092123--dc23/eng/20220406
LC record available at https://lccn.loc.gov/2022011382
LC ebook record available at https://lccn.loc.gov/2022011383

10 9 8 7 6 5 4 3 2 1

Published by Paraclete Press
Brewster, Massachusetts
www.paracletepress.com

Printed in the United States of America

CONTENTS

INTRODUCTION
Micah Mattix

T here has been a revival of Christian poetry in America, and our hope is
that this anthology will demonstrate as much by presenting some of the
best poems by some of the best poets, established and new, over the past 50
years. But first: what exactly is Christian poetry?

This isn't an easy question to answer. In a talk titled "Christianity and
Literature," which was first published in 1939, C. S. Lewis remarks that the
subject "did not seem to admit of any discussion": "The rules for writing a good
passion play or a good devotional lyric are simply the rules for writing tragedy
or lyric in general: success in sacred literature depends on the same qualities
of structure, suspense, variety, diction, and the like which secure success in
secular literature."[1] In other words, in terms of technique and form, there is
no such thing as Christian literature. There is simply good literature and bad
literature. As Lewis puts it: "Boiling an egg is the same process whether you are
a Christian or a Pagan."

Lewis goes on to state, however, that while there is no such thing as Christian
literature "*proprement dite*," there may be such a thing as a "Christian approach
to literature," which differs from what he calls the "modern" approach in one
important way. The modern approach values originality, which is conceived in
terms of breaking with convention and spontaneous self-expression: "I do not
know whether we often think out the implication of such language into a
consistent philosophy," Lewis remarks, "but we certainly have a general picture
of bad work flowing from conformity and discipleship, and of good work
bursting out from certain centers of explosive force—apparently self-originating
force—which we call men of genius."[2] But a Christian approach to literature
values imitation. Man is made in the image of God, Lewis writes, and he
"glorifies" God by "copying or imitating" him. This is because the universe is a
hierarchy where "some original divine virtue" is passed "downwards from rung
to rung" and where "the mode in which each lower rung receives it is . . .
imitation." A Christian approach to literature holds that "an author should
never conceive himself as bringing into existence beauty or wisdom which did
not exist before, but simply and solely as trying to embody in terms of his own

---

1 C. S. Lewis, "Christianity and Literature," *The Collected Works of C. S. Lewis* (New York:
Inspirational Press, 1996), 173.
2 Lewis, 174.

art some reflection of eternal Beauty and Wisdom."[3] Lewis's point here is an Augustinian one. In *De Doctrina*, Augustine argues that the Trinity is the only self-existent being. All other beings and things are dependent upon him for whatever existence they possess. To claim that art is original, in the proper sense of the word, Lewis suggests, is to claim that it has characteristics that did not exist previously, even in God.

While Lewis writes that a Christian theory of poetry is "above all . . . opposed to the idea that literature is self-expression," he is not claiming that Christian poets should not write about their own lives or draw from internal sources. He notes how the poet Phemius in the *Odyssey* claims to be both inspired by the gods and self-taught. Lewis asks: "How can he be self-taught if a god has taught him all he knows?" Lewis's answer is that the god's instruction was "internal" rather than "external" (that is, from other poets) and "is therefore regarded as part of the Self." But isn't this a kind of self-expression? No, according to Lewis, since Phemisus's self-expression transcends the self. He draws on internal sources to express something beyond himself, whereas, Lewis claims, fairly or not, modern writers see self-expression as an end in itself:

> A Christian poet and an unbelieving poet may both be equally original in the sense that they neglect the example of their poetic forbears and draw on resources particular to themselves, but with this difference. The unbeliever may take his own temperament and experience, just as they happen to stand, and consider them worth communicating simply be-cause they are facts or, worse still, because they are his. To the Christian his own temperament and experience, as mere fact, and as merely his, are of no value or importance whatsoever: he will deal with them, if at all, only because they are the medium through which, or the position from which, something universally profitable appeared to him.[4]

It is that "universally profitable" something that is the true subject of art for the Christian writer, according to Lewis, and it is in this sense that a Christian approach to literature should have no truck with art that is *merely* self-referential.

In arguing for the mimetic function of art, Lewis does not appear to deny its particularity, but he doesn't address this directly. He remarks that the Christian "will take literature a little less seriously than the cultured Pagan," but this is because the "cultured Pagan" takes literature much too seriously, making

---

3 Lewis, 177.
4 Lewis, 178.

art into something it is not, which, in turn, leads to a far more devastating diminishment. It is not only false to conceive of a poem as a self-referential and self-begetting artifact, but this concept of art has led to works of increasingly limited scope—preoccupied, first, with the power and authority of poetry itself as the only proper subject of poetry, followed by a lament of poetry's failure to be what it could have never been in the first place.[5] Lewis writes that "*a posteriori* it is hard to argue that all the greatest poems have been made by men who valued something else much more than poetry. . . . The real frivolity, the solemn vacuity, is all with those who make literature a self-existent thing to be valued for its own sake."[6] It is only when art is understood in its proper station with respect to God that it becomes most fully itself.

It is helpful to bring in Jacques Maritain here. As John C. Conley has noted, Maritain is hostile towards a mimetic theory of art that emphasizes material representation at the expense of spiritual representation.[7] In his brief discussion of Aristotle's mimetic theory in *Art and Scholasticism*, Maritain argues that it is wrong to take Aristotle's statement that all art is a form of imitation to mean that all art is an "exact reproduction or representation" of physical reality. Rather, mimesis is "to be understood here in the most *formal* sense."[8] The task of the artist is not to imitate the actions and objects of the physical world. If that were the case, Maritain writes, "it would have to be said that except for the art of the cartographer or the draughtsman of anatomical plates there is no imitative art."[9] Rather, the task of the artist is to imitate the moral and spiritual laws at work in the world. To be preoccupied with figurative realism, in Maritain's view, reduced the artist's freedom to capture the forces at work in the world in a work's structure and movement. Cubism, for example, has shown that art "does not consist in imitating" the objects of the physical world "but in making, composing or constructing, *in accordance with the laws of the very object to be posited in being*" (my emphasis).[10] "Maritain conceives the purpose of art," Conley writes, "as the embodiment of a spiritual reality in a finite organization of matter. The quest to grasp and present the transcendental becomes the fundamental dynamic of the artist."[11]

---

5 See Ben Lerner, *The Hatred of Poetry* (New York: Farrar, Straus and Giroux, 2016).

6 Lewis, 179.

7 John J. Conley, SJ, "Imitating Nature: Maritain's Reservations Concerning Artistic Mimesis." *Reading the Cosmos: Nature, Science, and Wisdom,* edited by Giuseppe Butera (Notre Dame: American Maritain Association, 2012), 241-48.

8 Jacques Maritain, *Art and Scholasticism and The Frontiers of Poetry,* translated by Joseph W. Evans (Notre Dame: University of Notre Dame Press, 1974), 54.

9 Maritain, 59.

10 Maritain, 53.

11 Conley, 246.

Why Maritain held that material and spiritual mimeses were in opposition to one another is unclear. But despite his obvious differences with Lewis, Maritain's remark that mimesis is primarily formal is not categorically different from Lewis's argument that the task of the artist is to "*embody in terms of his own art* some reflection of eternal Beauty and Wisdom" (my emphasis). But is mimesis a characteristic of a distinctly Christian literature, even if it is first proposed explicitly in Aristotle and has affinities with the Homeric idea of the poet as a "pensioner of the Muse," as Lewis puts it, and the Platonic theory of forms? Or, as with the case with formal unity, is it simply a characteristic of all literature, with the better works embracing it and the lesser ones attempting to avoid it?

In his magisterial *Mimesis: The Representation of Reality in Western Literature*, Erich Auerbach argues that the "figural realism" first used by Dante in *The Divine Comedy* is distinctly "Christian in spirit and Christian in origin."[12] This was a combination of two kinds of mimesis that Auerbach identified in his famous first chapter, "Odysseus's Scar"—the material realism of the "Homeric style" and the symbolism of Genesis. In the *Odyssey*, everything is "scrupulously externalized and narrated," Auerbach writes. He takes the example of the discovery of Odysseus's scar—and, hence, his identity—by his old housekeeper, Euryclea. In the scene, everything is clearly "outlined, brightly and uniformly illuminated, men and things stand out in a realm where everything is visible."[13] Feelings and thoughts are all clearly expressed. How Odysseus got his scar is explained in detail. There is no background. Everything is foreground. The purpose of this kind of description and narration is to create a scene that is fully present, "visible and palpable in all their parts, and completely fixed in their spatial and temporal relations."[14] All of the scenes are connected in such a way, Auerbach writes, that "their relationships—their temporal, local, causal, final, consecutive, comparative, concessive, antithetical, and conditional limitations—are brought to light in perfect fullness." The result is that "a continuous rhythmic procession of phenomena passes by, and never is there a form left fragmentary or half-illuminated, never a lacuna, never a gap, never a glimpse of unplumbed depths."[15]

The style of the Old Testament, however, which offers an equally epic account of a civilization, is completely different. Auerbach focuses on Genesis 22 in which we have the story of God commanding Abraham to sacrifice his

---

12 Erich Auerbach, *Mimesis: The Representation of Reality in Western Literature*, translated by Willard R. Trask (Princeton: Princeton University Press, 2014), 198.
13 Auerbach, 3.
14 Auerbach, 6.
15 Auerbach, 6-7.

son, Isaac. Where is God when he speaks to Abraham? We are not told. "He does not come, like Zeus or Poseidon, from the Aethiopians, where he has been enjoying a sacrificial feast," Auerbach writes, "Nor are we told anything of his reasons for tempting Abraham . . . unexpected and mysterious, he enters the scene from some unknown height or depth and calls."[16] We do not have an account of Abraham's response to God's request other than "Here I am" and his obedience. We are told nothing of the journey, other than it took three days. There is no account of Isaac's thoughts other than his one question about the animal for the sacrifice. "Only what we need to know about him as a personage in the action, here and now, is illuminated, so that it may become apparent how terrible Abraham's temptation is, and that God is fully aware of it."[17] Unlike the *Odyssey*, the details of the story have the function of increasing the narrative tension. Auerbach writes that in the biblical account of Abraham's sacrifice only phenomena that are needed to gesture toward some meaning are recounted; "all else" is "left in obscurity." The characters of the Old Testament are "multilayered," time and place are symbolic, and actions are fraught with moral significance. In Homer's poems, Auerbach writes, "Delight in physical existence is everything. . . . Their highest aim is to make that delight perceptible to us. . . . Homeric poems conceal nothing, they contain no teaching and no secret second meaning. Homer can be analyzed . . . but he cannot be interpreted."[18] The stories of the Old Testament, however, are "oriented toward truth"—a "tyrannical" truth, in Auerbach's view, since it excludes all other truths. "Far from seeking, like Homer, merely to make us forget our own reality for a few hours, it seeks to overcome our reality: we are to fit our own life into its world, feel ourselves to be elements in its structure of universal history."[19]

These two modes were combined in Dante's *Divine Comedy*, Auerbach argues, which is characterized by a "figural realism." Both Tertullian and Augustine defended the "historical reality" of biblical characters, Auerbach writes, "against all attempts at spiritually allegorical interpretation." They read characters such as Adam and Moses as both historical *and* allegorical, not merely one or the other. "Medieval symbolism and allegorism are often, as we know, excessively abstract," Auerbach continues, "and many traces of this are to be found in the Comedy itself. But far more prevalent in the Christian life of the High Middle ages is the figural realism which can be observed in full bloom in sermons, the plastic arts, and mystery plays . . . and it is this figural

16 Auerbach, 8.
17 Auerbach, 10-11.
18 Auerbach, 13.
19 Auerbach, 15.

realism which dominates Dante's view."[20] In other words, Dante's characters in *The Divine Comedy* speak and act, to a greater or lesser degree, like humans, which is captured, Auerbach argues, in an epic style balancing exposition and concision that surpasses both Homer and Virgil. Yet, these characters are also symbolic of something else—the intellectual pride of heresy, intemperance, selfishness, the beauty of charity, and so forth.

Auerbach's strict Hegelianism can lead him to make overly stark distinctions. The *Odyssey* can be interpreted, not just analyzed. The poem does more than make "delight perceptible to us." But it seems uncontroversial to say that a work of art in the Christian view is inherently double—both surface and depth, material and immaterial. It is both itself, functioning according to its own rules, and a reflection, or gesture towards, something else. This isn't to say that only Christians view art in this way, but over the last century there has been a movement away from this idea and a movement towards (or back to) a purely materialistic understanding of art. The revival of Christian poetry in America is, in part, a reaction against this anti-symbolic tendency.

⚜⚜⚜⚜⚜⚜

When T. S. Eliot was awarded the 1948 Nobel Prize for Literature, the committee unsurprisingly cited *The Waste Land*, with "its complicated symbolic language, its mosaic-like technique, and its apparatus of erudite allusion," as one reason for his selection. The other poem it singled out was *Four Quartets*. Anders Österling, the permanent secretary of the Swedish Academy at the time, praised the poem's "meditative music of words, with almost liturgical refrains and fine, exact expressions" of religious experience. Österling went on to argue that the two poems, so seemingly different, were of a piece: "His earliest poetry, so convulsively disintegrated, so studiously aggressive in its whole technical form, can finally also be apprehended as a negative expression of a mentality which aims at higher and purer realities and must first free itself of abhorrence and cynicism. In other words, his revolt is that of the Christian poet."[21] Russell Kirk saw the continuity between the earlier and later Eliot, too. In *Eliot and His Age*, he writes that *The Waste Land*'s assemblage of a "grander style and a purer vision in other centuries" casts light on our "parlous condition of abnormality": "*The Waste Land* is the endeavor of a philosophical poet to examine the life we

---

20 Auerbach, 196.
21 Anders Österling, "Presentation Speech." *Nobel Lectures, Literature: 1901-1967*, edited by Horst Frenz (New Jersey: Elsevier, 1969), 432.

live, relating the timeless to the temporal. A Seeker explores the modern Waste Land, putting questions into our heads; and though the answers we obtain may not please us, he has roused us from our death-in-life."[22]

The view that *The Waste Land* was preparatory—an expression of the vacuity of life without "higher and purer realities" that was necessary in order to turn back to those higher realities—might be read as a statement of the poem's inferiority, but that would be a mistake. The poem, rather, asks a question, as Kirk suggests, that *Four Quartets* will answer. That question is this: How can the old symbols and hierarchies (of presence over absence, order over disorder) possess so much beauty and power—particularly when compared to the flatness of a secular age—and simultaneously be merely illusory? The answer for Eliot was that the symbols are not illusory at all but real.

What followed Eliot, however, was a sustained attack on symbolism and meaning. In the early poetry of Wallace Stevens, for example, poetry is a beautiful game—sensuous and sonorous—but a game nonetheless. Poetry does not point to some higher order but instead creates a temporary one out of musicality and a play of particulars. Later in life, Stevens wondered if poetry's order wasn't something received from a higher one rather than an arbitrary one created by the poet—"God and the imagination are one," he wrote in 1951. But it was the early Stevens that captured the attention of younger poets, who were also inspired by the seemingly anti-symbolic work of William Carlos Williams and new ideas from France that conceived of language as entirely self-referential.

The history of American poetry in the twentieth century is complex, but one major development is the diminishment of the idea of poetry as symbol. Responding, in part, to the work of John Ashbery and Frank O'Hara, poets like Clark Coolidge, Charles Bernstein, and Bob Perelman, among others, wrote poetry that called into question art's capacity to reflect "reality." Language does not represent feelings. It constructs feelings that benefit those in power. We see this idea expressed clearly in Ron Silliman's fascinating but misguided 1987 essay "The New Sentence." For Silliman, the function of language is purely political—in *Linguistics and Economics*, Silliman writes, Ferroccio Rossi-Landi shows that "language use arises from the need to divide labor in the community."[23] A sentence is a tool that increases the means of production, but over time this purely material function was obscured by those in power in order to refigure language as mimetic—-something that represented reality rather

---

22 Russell Kirk, *Eliot and His Age* (Dover: ISI, 2008), 67-8.
23 Ron Silliman, "The New Sentence." *The New Sentence* (New York: Roof Books, 1987), 78.

than something that constructed it—in order to make the market economy seem natural and consolidate power. The task of the poet in this view is to subvert the idea of language as symbol and make clear its constructivist nature by breaking the sentence into fragments, excluding context, and undermining syntactical hierarchy through parataxis, among other things. The use of some of these techniques, though without the serious philosophical commitments of writers like Silliman, has become *de rigueur* for young MFA graduates trying to gain the attention of publishers and university search committees who have an economic interest in appearing "cutting edge." So much so, in fact, that Stephen Burt could refer to them, tongue partially in cheek, as a "school"—"Elliptical Poets"—in a 1998 piece for *Boston Review:* "Elliptical poets try to manifest a person—who speaks the poem and reflects the poet—while using all the verbal gizmos developed over the last few decades to undermine the coherence of speaking selves. They are post-avant-gardist, or post-'postmodern': they have read (most of them) Stein's heirs, and the 'language writers,' and have chosen to do otherwise." What Burt means by "otherwise" is "they want to entertain us as thoroughly as, but not to resemble, television."[24] They want to return, in Auerbach's terms, to a poetry that is all foreground and no background, that is all surface and no depth, that captures only the flux of the present.

It is unsurprising that Christian writers might react against this flat view of poetry by turning to figuration, form, and narrative. Poets like Robert B. Shaw, Dana Gioia, Andrew Hudgins, and Mark Jarman, among others, have turned to the examples of Donne and Eliot, Robert Frost and Richard Wilbur, to create works of formal and narrative complexity. It is because of the distinctly Christian understanding of art as mimetic, broadly conceived, that the return to form in the United States beginning in the 1970s and 1980s has been largely, though not exclusively, a Christian one. At the same time, poets like Shane McCrae have drawn *from* the post-structuralist critique of language as pure representation to show how the West has suppressed the voices and experiences of the marginalized. The subversion one finds in his work is a distinctly Christian kind of subversion, where the poet speaks for the silenced minority and shows how the culturally determined language of Western Christianity *can* be just that—culturally determined—rather than a faithful representation of the ethic found in the Old Testament and the Gospels. Still others, like Scott Cairns, have shown how language always falls short of reflecting the totality of anything, in particular the person of God himself, who cannot be contained by the finite.

---

24 Stephen Burt, Rev. of Susan Wheeler, *Smokes. Boston Review* (Summer 1998), par. 1.

One point, in fact, that post-structuralism shares with Christianity is this very idea that language, as powerful as it is, cannot contain all of reality. Words always leave something out. Some aspect of the relationship between things goes unsaid. There is an element of mystery in life that cannot be resolved in speech and text. In "Pilgrims," a poem about a visit to a small church, Robert B. Shaw writes that "Words are prone to blur in the fervent yearning / broadcast from the louvered bottom panes / of those embattled-looking pointy windows." Clare Rossini writes in "Prayer of Sorts" that "all words / Are yoked to the mute." "There's nothing," Bruce Beasley writes in "Doxology, " the heavens haven't uttered / already in shudders / of animation more firm than words." Yet, imperfect as it is, language itself always turns us towards this mystery. "Pick up any language by the scruff of its neck," Jeanne Murray Walker writes in "Staying Power," "wipe its face, set it down on the lawn, / and I bet it will toddle right into the godfire / again." Whatever one thinks of the "linguistic turn" of the twentieth century, it has been one that has sparked, rather than extinguished, religious poetry.

What has been unexpected is that so many gifted poets should write openly religious work that would be published in major trade and university presses— and that one of those volumes, Franz Wright's *Walking to Martha's Vineyard*, which begins with an apology for the existence of God, should win the Pulitzer Prize in 2004. In an introductory note to *Christianity and Literature*'s 2009 special issue on "Christianity and Contemporary Poetry," Julia Spicher Kasdorf (who is also included in this volume), suggests that the fragmentation of poetry in America post-WWII, where one encountered the work of Bernstein and Silliman alongside the confessional work of the poetic heirs of Robert Lowell and Sylvia Plath, the activist poetry of Amiri Baraka and June Jordan, and the musically vernacular work of Yusef Komunyakaa, has created a space for Christian poetry to develop along its own (multiple) lines. Contemporary poetry is now "as mongrel as anything else truly American," Kasdorf writes, and Christianity does well in mongrel times.[25]

No art flourishes without institutional support, however, and Christian poetry in America has benefited not only from the country's network of hundreds of Christian colleges and universities, which is without parallel in the contemporary West, but also from religious magazines like *First Things*, *The Christian Century*, *Commonweal*, *America*, *Plough Quarterly*, and *Books & Culture*, among others, who have all always included original poetry in their

---

25 Julia Spicher Kasdorf, "From the Poetry Editor." *Christianity and Literature* 58.4 (Summer 2009), 574.

pages. *Image Journal*, started by Gregory Wolfe in 1989, was and continues to be a major source of support for Christian writers, as are religious publishing houses like Paraclete, Eerdmans, St. Augustine's Press, Wipf & Stock, Angelico, Wiseblood, and Loyola, among others.

The result has been a rich and varied body of work. In addition to the return to form and narrative in works of Shaw and Gioia, Maryann Corbett and David Middleton, we have poets like Diane Glancy and Marilyn Nelson, who have incorporated the voices and syntax of African-Americans and Native Americans to create work that is both historically rich and strikingly fresh. Paul Mariani and James Matthew Wilson, among others, have used the confessional mode of Lowell in different ways to communicate what Lewis calls some "universally profitable" thing. Julia Spicher Kasdorf turns to the language of the Mennonite tradition as she explores the value and limits of communities in her work. Marly Youmans is indebted to the language of folk myths to create work that is both thoroughly contemporary and otherworldly. The "cracked" soul is of particular interest to poets as varied as Andrew Hudgins and Bruce Beasley. Both Shaw and Tracy K. Smith treat in various ways the intersection of science and faith. We have the devotional poems on the lives of the saints and biblical characters in the work of William Baer and Timothy Murphy. In the poetry of Brett Foster and Ryan Wilson we have work that is steeped in Donne and Herbert and, at the same time, thoroughly modern in its grittiness. John Poch and Benjamin Myers take on life in Texas and Oklahoma respectively in a way that transcends mere regionalism. Doubt is a touchstone of faith for Christian Wiman. While writing from various denominational backgrounds—Catholic, Presbyterian, Charismatic, Orthodox, Baptist—these Christian poets both praise the beauty of the universal Church and critique its failings and excesses. Far from uniform, the work of the poets in this volume is as varied as contemporary poetry itself while, at the same time, profoundly committed to a common faith.

<hr/>

The usefulness of an anthology is determined in part by its exclusions. Some of these are arbitrary, and some, the hope is, draw attention to something worth noticing by isolating it. In this volume, we have started with poets born in or after 1940, not because the date is inherently significant, but because one has to start somewhere, and we wanted to draw attention to mostly living poets who are still active today. This has meant excluding poets like Luci Shaw, Catherine

Savage Brosman, Wendell Berry, and Fred Chappell, among others, which some readers will no doubt find lamentable. Gifted poets like Wilmer Mills, who was born in 1969, but who died over 10 years ago, were also excluded. We have focused on American poets, however, because something has happened in this country in terms of a return to Christian verse, as noted above, and because including great international anglophone poets like the late Geoffrey Hill or Les Murray would have made the volume unwieldy.

We have also decided to focus on poems that, for the most part, treat matters of Christian doctrine and practice directly. There are a great many contemporary poets whose work is "spiritual" or whose faith is implicit rather than explicit in their work. These include poets like Louise Erdrich, Carolyn Forché, Li-Young Lee, Margaret Gibson, Gregory Orr, Martha Serpas, and Aaron Belz, among many others. Some readers may find this odd, but there are already a number of anthologies that gather many of these poets, and we wanted to do what few, if any, anthologies of contemporary poetry have yet to do—gather poems that are distinctly Christian in subject matter.

This volume in no way provides a comprehensive picture of contemporary Christian poetry in America. It is a selective volume, with significant selections from and substantial introductions to the work of major figures in the field. But the hope is that it is still a representative one, capturing something of the diverse styles and interests of Christian poets in this country, and one that has space for poets whose work, we believe, deserves more attention. As with any anthology, the volume is limited by the tastes and interests of the editors. Our hope is that readers will not allow this to distract them from the many pleasures and wisdom of the work included.

Paul Mariani (1940)

The sacramental imagination has, as Paul Mariani writes in his 2020 literary memoir *The Mystery of It All*, through two millennia of Christian tradition, "informed, reformed, and transformed what we read and see and understand about the entire spectrum of humanity." Mariani's literary language is inseparable from the Eucharistic language of his Catholic faith: the Christian writer's vision, wherever it turns its gaze, beholds in the created world the Real Presence of the divine imagination, immanent as well as transcendent. It is a vision both *there*, looking heavenward, and *here*, rooted in a fallen world where God nevertheless is never absent.

This vision informs Mariani's work as critic, literary biographer, and poet. Steeped in the work of other poets, chiefly such predecessors as Wallace Stevens, William Carlos Williams, Hart Crane, John Berryman, and his particular lodestar, Gerard Manley Hopkins, Mariani discerns the threads of sacramental vision in the complex fabric of each poet's body of work. His own poems, meanwhile, synthesize the influences of these predecessors: the modernist concern, for example, particularly a preoccupation for Williams, with generating in poetry a language that is vividly and uniquely American. Mariani's poems reflect something of the "Henry" of John Berryman's *Dream Songs*, whose emotional range encompasses anger, doubt, and despair, but also jokiness, as he wrestles, Jacob-like, with the presence, or absence, of God.

Unlike Berryman's wrestling, however, Mariani's poetic sensibility comes down always on the side of presence. Like Hopkins's, Mariani's poems occupy themselves with the *inscape* of created things: the presence in them that is at once the distilled essence of what they are and the sacramental presence of their Creator. Like Hopkins's, these poems record instances of *instress*, the revelation and apprehension of the divine presence, *there* and *here* at once, which underwrites the Christian understanding of reality. Implicit in this understanding, of course, is the recognition that *here* is not *there*, despite the abiding presence of God. The ways of God remain a mystery, even as those ways infuse and shape human ends. Still, as human ends are inscribed, by God, as matter for his care, so they are inscribed, by the poet, as matter for poetry.

A poem like "Quid Pro Quo," for example, can traverse a wide terrain of fallen, timebound human experience. The poem begins with a miscarriage. In his anger, the bereft father gives God the middle finger, only later to receive a son, given like the biblical Isaac after that hopeless barren season. This son in his own season offers himself at the altar to receive holy orders, putting on, sacramentally, the person of Christ, victim and priest. In the trajectory of this poem, concerned as it is with things of this world—one man's grief, anger, and marveling—the whole mysterious sweep of salvation history is encompassed. What undergirds even the man's impotent rage is, in Mariani's own words, "a foundational sacredness," in which "God's imagination and the human imagination . . . mesh and fuse."

Paul Mariani was born in 1940 in New York City, the eldest of seven children. He received part of his secondary education at Beacon Marianist Prep, where he underwent a period of discernment for a priestly vocation in that order, later graduating from Mineola

High School. His subsequent education included an undergraduate degree from Manhattan College and graduate degrees from Colgate University and the City University of New York. Over the course of a distinguished academic career, he has taught at Colgate University, the John Jay College of Criminal Justice, the University of Massachusetts, Boston College, and the Bread Loaf School of English. He has also served as a faculty member for numerous writers' conferences, notably the Bread Loaf Writers' Conference.

He is the author of eight books of poetry, most recently 2020's *Ordinary Time*. He has also published a commentary on the poetry of Gerard Manley Hopkins, as well as literary biographies of Hopkins, John Berryman, Robert Lowell, Hart Crane, and Wallace Stevens. In *God and the Imagination: Poetry, Poets, and the Ineffable* and *The Mystery of It All: The Vocation of Poetry in the Twilight of Modernism*, Mariani deals explicitly with the Christian imagination in poetry. He is also the author of *Thirty Days: On Retreat with St. Ignatius*, a meditation on the Spiritual Exercises of Saint Ignatius of Loyola. Mariani has received a Guggenheim Fellowship, multiple fellowships from the National Endowment for the Arts and the National Endowment for the Humanities, the John Ciardi Lifetime Achievement Award in Poetry, and the 2019 Flannery O'Connor Lifetime Achievement Award, presented by the Catholic Imagination Conference at Loyola University Chicago.

Quid Pro Quo

Just after my wife's miscarriage (her second
in four months), I was sitting in an empty
classroom exchanging notes with my friend,
a budding Joyce scholar with steel-rimmed
glasses, when, lapsed Irish Catholic that he was,
he surprised me by asking what I thought now
of God's ways toward man. It was spring,

such spring as came to the flint-backed Chenango
Valley thirty years ago, the full force of Siberia
behind each blast of wind. Once more my poor wife
was in the local four-room hospital, recovering.
The sun was going down, the room's pinewood panels
all but swallowing the gelid light, when, suddenly,
I surprised not only myself but my colleague

by raising my middle finger up to heaven, *quid
pro quo*, the hardly grand defiant gesture a variant

on Vanni Fucci's[26] figs, shocking not only my friend
but in truth the gesture's perpetrator too. I was 24,
and, in spite of having pored over the *Confessions*
& that Catholic Tractate called the *Summa*, was sure
I'd seen enough of God's erstwhile ways toward man.

That summer, under a pulsing midnight sky
shimmering with Van Gogh stars, in a creaking,
cedar-scented cabin off Lake George, having lied
to the gentrified owner of the boys' camp
that indeed I knew wilderness & lakes and could,
if need be, lead a whole fleet of canoes down
the turbulent whitewater passages of the Fulton Chain

(I who had last been in a rowboat with my parents
at the age of six), my wife and I made love, trying
not to disturb whosever headboard & water glass
lie just beyond the paper-thin partition at our feet.
In the great black Adirondack stillness, as we lay
there on our sagging mattress, my wife & I gazed out
through the broken roof into a sky that seemed

somehow to look back down on us, and in that place,
that holy place, she must have conceived again,
for nine months later in a New York hospital she
brought forth a son, a little Buddha-bellied
rumpelstiltskin runt of a man who burned
to face the sun, the fact of his being there
both terrifying & lifting me at once, this son,

this gift, whom I still look upon with joy & awe. Worst,
best, just last year, this same son, grown
to manhood now, knelt before a marble altar to vow
everything he had to the same God I had had my own
erstwhile dealings with. How does one bargain
with a God like this, who, *quid pro quo*, ups
the ante each time He answers one sign with another?

---

26 In Dante's *Inferno*, a thief inhabiting the eighth circle of Hell, who makes obscene gestures with
his thumb and fingers—"figs," suggesting copulation—at God.

The Great Wheel

In the Tuileries we came upon the Great Wheel
rising gargantuan above the trees. Evening
was coming on. An after-dinner stroll, descending
by easy stages toward the river, a bridge of leaves
above us, broken here and there by street lights
coming on. Our time here nearly over, our return

home a shadow hovering. Paris, city of returns,
you said, for the pleasure of it, like the Great Wheel
looming there above us, all steel & light
& music, daredevil daunting, against the evening
sky with the tower in the distance winking. The leaves
still held firmly, the unthinkable descending

of what lay ahead undreamt of still, death descending
inevitably as the Great Wheel in its return,
(a descent first through summer's golden leaves
and then bare ruined branches), the Great Wheel
turning & returning. As then, with the all but evening
over us, our wives laughing by the entrance lights,

we rose above the mansard roofs, the trees, the lights,
lifting in a vertiginous ascent before descending,
as we chattered on against the coming on of evening,
our seat creaking in the rising wind, anxious to return
now to earth's solidities. Instead, the Great Wheel
merely sighed and lifted, stopping at the top, leaving

each of us alone now with our thoughts. The leaves
below, green, gray-green, gray, the dollhouse roofs, lights
like diamonds winking, aloof & distant, the Great Wheel
playing us, two middle-aged men, each descending
toward the Wheel's one appointed end, the Great Return
to earth, as the books all have it, come our evening.

For all our feigned bravado, we could feel the evening
over us, even as we stared down upon the blur of leaves,
our wives, our distant children, on all we would return

to, the way shipwrecked sailors search for lights
along a distant shore, as we began the last descent,
leaving the tents and Garden with its Great Wheel

to return, my dear dead friend, to the winking lights
along the boulevard, leaves lifting & descending,
as now the evening air took mastery, it & the Great Wheel.

Mother of Consolation

What you look hard at looks back hard at you.
As in this icon, where the child with the deer-
brown eyes gazes at something just beyond your view,
this child king who spreads blessing everywhere.

Blood of his mother's blood, bone of her bone.
Identical the mouth, the nose, the eyes.
You can see he is his mother's son, and hers alone,
in any way one's DNA supplies.

If too he is his Father's Son, how can you know
but by what burns behind the gaze, or in
the innocence of blessing? And even then there's no
way to know until you touch the mystery within.

And for that you will have first to understand
what it is you gaze at with the same dim eyes
too long glutted on the sensual, the bland,
the million million flyspecked buzzing lies.

The scrim of sight is dimmed with sick desire.
The Buddha knew this, and Blake, and Dante too.
How hard, O how very hard to re-ignite the fire,
the inner flame that lets us look upon these two,

These two whose gaze gives back peace again,
but only if we learn to turn the outward gaze into
the gaze within, the child's eyes remembering the When,
the mother's doe-brown eyes as she turns to gaze at you.

HOLY SATURDAY

A dream the old song has it, just
a dream. I was driving the old beige
Camry going round and around
and around searching for the Jeep
I was sure I'd parked or would have parked
near the decaying wharfs down by the sea
the day before but unable now
to find it though I kept circling back
And forth and back alley after alley
without any luck then finally thought
To press the panic button on my key
fob and yes I thought I could just
make out the beep beep sound
so that I had to believe my car
was waiting out there somewhere
as now fog and night descended.
It was then I remember seeing two
middle-aged women sitting in an old
van one at the foot the other at the head
so I rolled down my window to ask
if they could hear the beep beep
and if they could would they please
please be good enough to tell me
where the signal was coming from
because as I explained my hearing
wasn't very good now and I couldn't tell
if I was even headed in the right direction.
They were friendly enough and both
smiled back at me and asked if it was
a pizza truck or an ambulance
I was looking for or if the thing
was red or white the whole time
these pleasant smiles fitted to their faces
until it dawned on me that I would have to
keep on searching by myself though by now
everything was dark and the signal I was sure

I'd heard I think kept growing dimmer
though it had to be out there oh God
it had to be out there somewhere
still waiting for me to find it.

WHAT HAPPENED THEN

Do we understand what happened then?
The few of us in that shuttered room,
lamps dimmed, afraid of what would happen
when they found us? The women back
this morning to tell Peter what they'd seen.
Then these two back from Emmaus.
And now here he was. Here in the room with us.
Strange meeting this, the holes there
in his hands and feet and heart.
And who could have guessed a calm like this
could touch us? But that was what we felt.
The deep relief you feel when the one
you've searched for in a crowd appears,
and your unbelieving eyes dissolve in tears.
For this is what love looks like and is
and what it does. "Peace" was what he said,
as a peace like no other pierced the gloom
and descended on the room.

Diane Glancy (1941)

Diane Glancy is of Native American and British-German descent. She was born and raised in Kansas City, Missouri, but had little interaction with her father's Cherokee family. Her father never spoke about his heritage—"He faced the past with silence," she said in an interview for *Image*—and it was not until she moved to Oklahoma in 1964 after she graduated from the University of Missouri that she began to connect with that heritage and later explore it in her poetry. In collections such as *Brown Wolf Leaves the Res*, *Iron Woman*, *Asylum in the Grasslands*, and *Primer of the Obsolete*, Glancy takes on the voice of native characters in a highly inventive vocabulary to tell the story of her people.

"Poetry itself is memory," Glancy said in a 2019 interview for *Literary Hub*, but memory is "a creator as well as rememberer." In *The Book of Bearings*, for example, Glancy creates a character called Saint Bo-gast-ah to speak what she feels is missing in the diaries of Catharine Brown, a Cherokee teacher at the Brainerd Mission who died in 1823. Where Brown's diaries are "stiff with artificiality," Glancy's Bo-gast-ah speaks frankly of the violence of assimilation—"They covered our world and turned us by force to theirs"—but also of the grace that came with it. "Any culture that has undergone assimilation is not happy," Glancy told *Image*. "Imagine a foreign country imposing itself over your land. . . . Yet the positive aspect was that salvation came through assimilation." While Bo-gast-ah records the many losses of the Native American peoples, she also cries out to the God, with whom she now identifies, who also arrived with the white man:

> Have mercy on the uprooted.
> On the unwanted.
> On the made-over to fit somehow.
> You reform us, Lord.
> You yourself were remade to a man struggling
> on the cross.
> You were thought odd.
> You were dismissed.
> In that we are one.

"I see a continuum between scripture and Native belief," Glancy has remarked, and in poems like "Doot Dah Do" and "Holy Ghost," which are included below, Glancy retells the story of the Fall and the comments on the agency of the third person in the Trinity in an imagined native idiom that reframes the God of the Bible as the Cherokee Great Spirit.

Glancy grew up attending the local Methodist church. In her memoir, *The Dream of a Broken Field*, she writes that while attending church did not affect her family life at all, she was confirmed there but later left it for a period of time for a Pentecostal church: "I came to Christ in a Methodist church, then left because I was a zealot according to their standards.

Christ is Lord, I proclaimed at the altar. It was too much for them. I found a church outside the Methodist church. A fundamental, Pentecostal church, wherein I found the strength to walk through the fire. Or the Holy One who walked with me had strength to walk through the fire. I simply followed."

Glancy is professor emerita at Macalester College in St. Paul, Minnesota, and was the Richard R. L. Thomas Chair in Creative Writing at Kenyon College from 2008 to 2009. She is the author of over 30 books of poems, over 20 novels, and several plays. She has received many prizes for her work, including the Juniper Prize for Poetry, the Oklahoma Book Award, the Pablo Neruda Prize for Poetry, the American Book Award, the Minnesota Book Award in Poetry, and the Native American Prose Award, among others. She was awarded the Cherokee Medal of Honor by the Cherokee Honor Society and is a recipient of a National Endowment for the Arts grant and a Sundance Screenwriting Fellowship.

Doot Dah Do

Once the earth was new
and all the animals still shiny,
the cellophane hardly off them,
the tags still stuck on.
They squeaked funny new sounds.
And man was new, still wet in places.
He named the animals,
said *lets do already lets*.
So they did their dooed and died
and the Great Spirit sorrowed over the dooed
they did.
He created them so He could talk to someone,
you know how it is to be the Great Spirit,
if you've ever been disappointed and alone,
that's what it's like.
Only He has the power, of course,
to make things talk,
the power to shut them up,
the power you know to make the rain.
Then afterwards men were new again,
the animals by two this time,
but men still said *lets do*
and did their dooed and died again.

So the Great Spirit said *nuf.*
He made Chief Jesus to died for them
so they would not forever
in their died state dooed.
But they sent him back with holes in His hands
from their campsite which dogs guard and bit.
They said, *let's dooed* and still they did,
but others saw the bite holes
and became new dooders
and plugged him in and stopped
dunning the dooed they did.

Why I Like God

stay out late He says
do whatever you want
wear My shield and helmet anytime
nothing will get you
not even those *squeaky* nights
fly between the surfboards of My wings
say *I come from a pit I stand on a rock*
pike a torpedo into the sky
light as a sharp trombone
paste the metal body of My plane
you can fly to My yard
dry when you land
sometimes clear
sometimes abundant with wind-changed
flocks of sheep
their shifting migrations over the earth
are shapes you can fly through
if you want
straight to the sliver of the moon
crawling through the sky on its hands and toes.

Holy Ghost

All their hosts shall fall down
   —Isaiah 34:4

Holy Ghost wears furry chaps and a grapevine belt,
a red shirt and a cowboy hat.
He owns the marina by the river.
Hopscotch is his game.
But the clouds are his too.
Most days they are too heavy to let him off the ground.
He stays at the marina selling bait.
He sets a barrel fire to light Father's message.
He comforts the customers.
Holy Ghost prophesies for the Son's sake
with a string of words in another tongue.
He tells the Father's stories.
Comets full of ice once fell to earth and delivered the oceans
so Father could sail.
Their impact made the ocean beds.
The heavens are still falling.
Maple leaves splay on the walk like wrecked stars.

Jeanne Murray Walker (1944)

Among contemporary American poets, Jeanne Murray Walker emerges as a postmodern heir to the English metaphysical poets of the seventeenth century. Like her literary forebear George Herbert, Walker meditates continually on the strange mercy of God, which in the crush and cruelty of his creation reveals itself in improbable ways. Like Herbert, too, Walker is a lover of paradox. The central paradox of her poems: where God is most absent, there God is. Even as the speaker in her poem "Staying Power" renounces belief—"all right, it is improbable, all right, there / is no God"—God appears, as if summoned to a burning bush by that very act of unbelief. "[A]s if I'm focusing / a magnifying glass on dry leaves, God blazes up."

Like Herbert, meanwhile, Walker can arrange a complex meditation on human frailty and the radical mercy of God around a striking conceit. In "Little Blessing for My Floater," for example, a poem "after George Herbert," a blind spot in the eye both recalls and expands upon the biblical mote of Matthew 7:3. In the Gospel, Christ invokes the mote, or speck, in the eye, as a figure for sin: someone else's sin, which the sinner wishes to address while ignoring his own. Unlike this biblical sinner, the speaker in Walker's poem is aware of the speck in her own eye, and aware, further, of its metaphorical import. It negates the objects of her vision, even as sin itself is a negation, a cancellation of the human soul. This blind spot becomes a flashpoint for epiphany:

> I embrace you, piece of absence
> that reminds me what I will be,
> all dark some day unless God
> rescues me, oh speck
> that might teach me yet to see.

Walker's poems explore, too, her fascination with language: how human language, image of the Logos, can turn itself inside-out in its quest to articulate something true that exists beyond the capacity of language to express. The vocation of these poems is to make manifest, as in the penultimate line of "In the Beginning Was the Word," "creation thinking about itself." Her body of work meditates on women's work of childbirth and child-rearing, on women's invisible presences in history, on the unsung efforts of a high-school English teacher who "had to teach us everything," all participating in an ongoing labor of creation.

These meditations reflect the metaphysical poet's vision of something beyond the material world, imposing an unseen order, logic, and meaning on the chaos of that world, which it is the poet's charism to discern. The English teacher of "Light," for example— Mr. Luman, whose name recalls, inexactly, the Latin noun *lumen*—adopts something like entropy as a standing lesson plan. "He vowed to donate ten thousand dollars / to whichever of us named our first kid / *Igor Stravinsky* . . . He begged us not to smoke, to see the *Nutcracker*." Burdened with the self-imposed task of ensuring the survival of civilization as he knows it, Mr. Luman teaches by hurling the entropic contents of his mind into the void of the classroom, hoping perhaps in vain that something will stick to somebody. The poem's ending, in which Mr. Luman "met the train / at the blind crossing," suggests that he understands the futility of this hope, and has surrendered to despair. Yet the very disorder which characterizes his actions throughout the poem—"he dodged through / subjects like a bumper car at a carnival"—echoes the process by which light is generated, an explosion of photons from heated electrons, a wave, complex with moving particles, which emits from a source but has no discernible destination. Only at the distance provided by hindsight can the poem's speaker discern the shape of those waves and recognize the chaos as light.

Born in Parkers Prairie, Minnesota, in 1944, Jeanne Murray Walker is the author of nine books of poetry, numerous dramatic scripts, a memoir, *The Geography of Memory*, which chronicles the experience of caring for a parent with Alzheimer's, and *Pilgrim, You Find the Path by Walking*, a meditation on poetic form. Additionally, she is the editor, with Darryl Tippens, of an anthology, *Shadow and Light: Literature and the Life of Faith*. She taught for many years at the University of Delaware and in the low-residency Master of Fine Arts program in creative writing at Seattle Pacific University. Among her honors are a Pew Fellowship in the Arts, a fellowship from the National Endowment for the Arts, multiple Pennsylvania Council on the Arts Fellowships, and the Glenna Luschei-Prairie Schooner Prize. She has served as poetry editor for *Christianity and Literature*, and on the editorial boards of the literary journals *Image* and *Shenandoah*.

LIGHT

And then there was Mr. Luman, the teacher
whose death they announced one Tuesday.
He vowed to donate ten thousand dollars
to whichever of us named our first kid
Igor Stravinsky. We should send him a telegram,
he said. He'd cut off his thumbs for culture.
He'd be happy to dive five stories naked
from the window of English to make us
understand "To Be or Not to Be."
He knew we thought he had no life,
that he was a cardboard cutout
they wheeled from the closet every
morning. And really, what was he
but the longing he wanted to instill
in us for the finer things? He was nothing
but fumes that lingered after the last note

of the Brahms *Requiem.* He dodged through
subjects like a bumper car at a carnival.
He had to teach us everything!
He begged us not to smoke, to see *The Nutcracker.*
He claimed Hamlet was the only character
smart enough to have written the play he's in.
When the bell rang,
he was still talking about Queen Elizabeth,
how Lord Burghley brought a ten-pound note
to the coronation to buy back the British crown
from God, who is the true king.
We unfolded our bright limbs from his old desks
and filed past him to Math. The last thing
I heard him say before he met the train
at the blind crossing, was how in Egypt
when the dead knock to get into heaven
if their good deeds equal the weight
of one feather, they are let in.

LITTLE BLESSING FOR MY FLOATER
after George Herbert

This tiny ruin in my eye, small
flaw in the fabric, little speck
of blood in the egg, deep chip
in the windshield, north star,
polestar, floater that doesn't
float, spot where my hand is not,
even when I'm looking at my hand,
little piton that nails every rock
I see, no matter if the picture
turns to sand, or sand to sea,
I embrace you, piece of absence
that reminds me what I will be,
all dark some day unless God
rescues me, oh speck
that might teach me yet to see.

STAYING POWER

*In appreciation of Maxim Gorky at the International Convention
of Atheists, 1929*

Like Gorky, I sometimes follow my doubts
outside to the yard and question the sky,
longing to have the fight settled, thinking
I can't go on like this, and finally I say

all right, it is improbable, all right, there
is no God. And then as if I'm focusing
a magnifying glass on dry leaves, God blazes up.
It's the attention, maybe, to what isn't there

that makes the emptiness flare like a forest fire
until I have to spend the afternoon dragging
the hose to put the smoldering thing out.
Even on an ordinary day when a friend calls,

tells me they've found melanoma,
complains that the hospital is cold, I say God.
God, I say as my heart turns inside out.
Pick up any language by the scruff of its neck,

wipe its face, set it down on the lawn,
and I bet it will toddle right into the godfire
again, which—though they say it doesn't
exist—can send you straight to the burn unit.

Oh, we have only so many words to think with.
Say God's not fire, say anything, say God's
a phone, maybe. You know you didn't order a phone,
but there it is. It rings. You don't know who it could be.

You don't want to talk, so you pull out
the plug. It rings. You smash it with a hammer
till it bleeds springs and coils and clobbery
metal bits. It rings again. You pick it up

and a voice you love whispers hello.

THE SIGN

Give me a sign, I pray, and then I see
For Sale (Price Reduced) and I smile
at the Almighty's roguish sense of humor,

thinking after all he might not spurn skeptics,
stretching out his carpenter's hand
to let St. Thomas probe the nail holes,

stick his finger deep in the bleeding gash,
feel the spiky bones, and fly through
that little space to faith. Two thousand years

bereft of Jesus' body, I need a sign,
although I doubt that any sign could fix for good
how a God-man walked this curving earth.

And anyway, concerning signs, how childlike
my belief in narrative—as if, after the question,
the answer leaps up in perfect sequence.

Sequence, which is nothing but Time's
lackey! So I give up narrative, however lovely,
to scan the landscape. But I worry.

Suppose the sign arrived last week, for instance:
the spider threading sunlight by our garage,
a writhing knot of fire. Or last spring

in Carol's row of jewel-like tulips. Suppose
it was that rag of human song that drifted by
as we wandered Bleecker Street with Charlie,

just back from war. Or the muffled cracking
as my body bends under the press of time.
Not this, not that—I admit,

I'm down to rummaging the world
for nail holes. Maybe to list what's missing
is to start to understand what's here.

IN THE BEGINNING WAS THE WORD

It was your hunch, this world. On the heyday
of creation, you called, *Okay, go!* and a ball
of white-hot gasses spun its lonely way
for a million years, all spill and dangerous fall
until it settled into orbit. And a tough
neighborhood, it was, too. Irate Mars,
and sexually explicit Venus, the kerfluff
of a moody moon, and self-important stars.

And trees. Think of their endless rummaging
for light, their reckless greening, how flowering
is barely regulated damage. Then birds,
mice, sheep. Soon people, bursting into language.
Creation thinking about itself: our words soaring
like yours through time, dangerous, ordinary words.

THE CREATION

was going well. A perfect, rosy sow,
a finch, an elephant. Then a giraffe
at the last minute, springing up like Wow,
an exclamation point on legs. A gaff,
or maybe not. Her fringy eyelashes.
Her voice, a bleat soft as a low laugh,
a yard-long tongue that blackly licks leaf-caches
from the sky. She nuzzles her newborn calf,
still wet, eyes shut, legs splayed and sliding,
the two of them improbable riff-raff
of the imagination, hang gliding
off the cliff of reason.

Oh giraffes,
wear your head-lamps, gather around, remind me,
when all seems dark and sane, of mystery.

Marilyn Nelson (1946)

Marilyn Nelson's poetry is one of listening. Unlike many contemporary poets, she eschews her own life as subject matter ("I'm one of the lucky ones, with too happy a life for poetry," she tells Jeanne Murray Walker in an interview for *Image*) and instead assumes the voices of figures like Emmett Till and George Washington Carver, as well as silenced voices of the past, such as a slave whose remains were used for scientific experiments by his owner. "Poems come out of silence," Nelson tells Walker, "out of the accidental and intentional juxtaposition of combustible thoughts." At the same time, even the "accidental" is shaped by providence and form. The narrative of story, which we receive from a story-telling God, and the "intricate verbal structures" of poetic form not only contribute to creativity, Nelson has remarked, but lead poets "to discover things" that they might not otherwise discover.

Nelson's poetry is also one of witness. It testifies of the suffering of the oppressed and the brutality of oppressors without idolizing or demonizing either. In her poem "Churchgoing," for example, she recounts how an otherwise uninspiring worship service is transformed by the singing of the American spiritual "Were You There (When They Crucified My Lord)." Nelson writes that "This simple melody . . . captures exactly what I think faith is":

> That slaves should suffer in his agony!
> That Christian, slave-owning hypocrisy
> nevertheless was by these slaves ignored
> as they pitied the poor body of Christ!
> Oh, sometimes it causes me to tremble,
> that they believe most, who so much have lost.
> To be a Christian one must bear a cross.

Unlike Philip Larkin's "Church Going," which ends with an attempt to make intellectual sense of the poet's strange—and entirely secular—attraction to churches, Nelson's poem ends with spiritual warfare:

> I sit alone, tormented in my heart
> by fighting angels, one group black, one white.
> The victory is uncertain, but tonight
> I'll lie awake again, and try to start
> finding the black way back to what we've lost.

The "we" is significant, referring not only to African-American Christians but to all believers.

Nelson grew up in a military family and began attending a Lutheran church regularly as a teenager. She was involved in the Luther League, worked as an associate in the Lutheran Campus Ministry at Cornell University, and served on the Hymn Text Committee of the Lutheran Church in America. Nelson earned a BA from the University of California, Davis, an MA from the University of Pennsylvania, and a PhD from the University of Minnesota. She taught for many years at the University of Connecticut at Storrs and was the Poet Laureate of Connecticut from 2001 to 2006. She won the Ruth Lilly Poetry Prize from the Poetry Foundation and the Robert Frost medal. She is a three-time finalist for the National Book Award and the recipient of fellowships from the National Endowment for the Arts and the Guggenheim Foundation. She was Chancellor of the Academy of American Poets from 2013 to 2018.

Faith "is a gift," Nelson has remarked, but it is a gift that is received by listening. In her essay, "The Fruit of Silence," Nelson writes that meditation is an act of turning elsewhere while also turning inward. "I owe a great deal of my understanding of contemplative prayer from a former Benedictine," she writes in the essay, "a Catholic priest who now lives as a hermit and is the friend I've called 'Abba Jacob' in many poems. During one of several retreats he gave on Contemplative Prayer during his recent visit to the United States, 'Abba Jacob' said contemplation is simply a matter of focusing on a mantra while knowing that one is receiving oneself from and giving oneself back to a loving Creator." One of these Abba Jacob poems—"For the Feast of Corpus Christi"—is included in this volume.

CHURCHGOING
after Philip Larkin

The Lutherans sit stolidly in rows;
only their children feel the holy ghost
that makes them jerk and bobble and almost
destroys the pious atmosphere for those
whose reverence bows their backs as if in work.
The congregation sits, or stands to sing,
or chants the dusty creeds automaton.
Their voices drone like engines, on and on,
and they remain untouched by everything;
confession, praise, or likewise, giving thanks.
The organ that they saved years to afford
repeats the Sunday rhythms song by song,
slow lips recite the credo, smother yawns,

and ask forgiveness for being so bored.
I, too, am wavering on the edge of sleep,
and ask myself again why I have come
to probe the ruins of this dying cult.
I come bearing the cancer of my doubt
as superstitious suffering women come
to touch the magic hem of a saint's robe.

Yet this has served two centuries of men
as more than superstitious cant; they died
believing simply. Women, satisfied
that this was truth, were racked and burned with them
for empty words we moderns merely chant.

We sing a spiritual as the last song,
and we are moved by a peculiar grace
that settles a new aura on the place.
This simple melody, though sung all wrong,
captures exactly what I think is faith.
Were you there when they crucified my Lord?
That slaves should suffer in his agony!
That Christian, slave-owning hypocrisy
nevertheless was by these slaves ignored
as they pitied the poor body of Christ!
Oh, sometimes it causes me to tremble,
that they believe most, who so much have lost.
To be a Christian one must bear a cross.
I think belief is given to the simple
as recompense for what they do not know.

I sit alone, tormented in my heart
by fighting angels, one group black, one white.
The victory is uncertain, but tonight
I'll lie awake again, and try to start
finding the black way back to what we've lost.

INCOMPLETE RENUNCIATION

Please let me have
a 10-room house adjacent to campus;
6 bedrooms, 2½ baths, formal
dining room, frplace, family room,
screened porch, 2-car garage.
Well maintained.
And let it pass
through the eye of a needle.

FOR THE FEAST OF CORPUS CHRISTI
for Perry and Debbie

Songbirds skitter among the rafters,
scissoring in and out of the high stained windows.
Abba Jacob watches them a moment,
fingering through his tousled hair.
He looks at the gathered waiting,
cocks his head, smiles.

Today is the feast day of the mewling newborn in the hay,
the thirsty teacher wiping his brow, the dying man's iron grimace.
Today we celebrate a squalling toddler with a load in his pants,
a runny-nosed five-year-old, a boy with scabbed knees.
We celebrate Jesus, who suffered and died.
Who laughed, who sneezed, who scratched where he itched.
He did not live by bread alone,
but he lived by bread. And he liked
a cool drink of fresh-dipped water
drawn smiling from the well.
He tasted. He saw.
When he stepped out onto a wave his feet got muddy.
He faced forward as we do, with fingers-crossed faith.

Six rows from the door, Amma Mama notices
the island echolessness of the morning's songbirds.
She never dreamed, though she'd always somehow known,
she'd be here again, watching him spacegaze as he speaks.
Hearing him laugh. He described last night's dinner wine
as "masculine," explained that its taste was what
every man would like to be:
intelligent, handsome, reliable, and a little bit rough
around the edges. His voice, she thinks,
is almost sweeter than the birdsong.

As his body, the church, we remember
ourselves in our Eucharist,
giving thanks for the assurance
that we shall not end here.
Trekking through the desert of brevity toward this
shimmering Zion,
is it bread we eat, or manna?
Wine we drink, or dew?
We make Eucharist for the daily miracles
which sustain us: for food, drink, and fellowship,
for the promise of Christ.

The pause fills with twitter. Beyond faint surf,
vast silence.
Abba Jacob raises his eyebrows, shrugs.
If we are the body of Christ,
then our bodies are Christ's bodies, too, *non?*
Your bodies, mine.
A thousand years ago, exiled for his writings,
St. Simeon continued to describe indwelling light.
If we truly love Christ, he wrote, we inhabit Christ.
Every part of us, even the most secret, the parts we hide in shame,
every part becomes his, and is therefore healed, hallowed, beautiful
and radiant with loving light. When that happens, everything we see
we see gently, every word we speak listens, every act is reverent,
every caress is a blessing.

Around Amma Mama backs straighten, heads slowly nod.
His darklit eyes beacon the pews.
Those of you who have partners, who have vowed
a love without ceasing, when you lie together, make love
to the immeasurable mystery of spirit enfleshed.
Touch each other with Christ's touch.
Kiss each other with Christ's mouth.
Give to and receive from each other Christ's body.
Your fingers a sacrament of tenderness.

Blessing air pocked with gasps,
Abba Jacob says *Amen.*

MIRACLE IN THE COLLECTION PLATE
Rev. Christopher Rush, 1850

Brothers and sisters, we know why we're here
this evening. The sad news has traveled fast
of Brother James's capture. For three years
he lived amongst us, tasting happiness.[27]

His wife and child are here with us tonight.
God bless you, Sister. Without a goodbye,
James was handcuffed, and shoved on a steamboat
to Baltimore, to be sold—legally!

Neighbors, we know that upright, decent man:
James Hamlet: a loving husband, father, friend.

---

27 Nelson's note on this poem reads as follows: "In 1850 the U.S. Congress passed the Fugitive
Slave Law, which made any federal marshal or other official who did not arrest an alleged
runaway slave liable to a fine of $1,000. Law enforcement officials everywhere now had
a duty to arrest anyone suspected of being a runaway slave on no more evidence than a
claimant's sworn testimony of ownership. The suspected slave could not ask for a jury
trial or testify on his or her own behalf. In addition, any person aiding a runaway slave
by providing food or shelter was subject to six months' imprisonment and a $1,000 fine.
Officers who captured a fugitive slave were entitled to a bonus. Slave owners only needed to
supply an affidavit to a federal marshal to capture an escaped slave. This law led to many free
blacks being conscripted into slavery, as they had no rights in court and could not defend
themselves against accusations. James Hamlet was the first fugitive arrested under the new
law. His African American and Abolitionist friends raised the money necessary to purchase
his freedom."

Many of us would gladly risk the fine
or prison sentence, if we could help him.

My friends, all is not lost! It's not too late!
We are told that Brother James may be redeemed!
His buyer will sell him! But we cannot wait:
we need eight hundred dollars to free him.
Eight hundred. I know every penny counts,
living from widow's mite to widow's mite.
But with God's help, we can raise that enormous amount!
Let's make a miracle in the collection plate!

THE TEMPERANCE FLU

Nancy, negro servant of Mrs. Mary Ann Noyes,
excommunicated for drunkenness, First Congregational Church, Lyme,
CT, May, 1817

It seem like everybody got the temperance flu:
it's a epidemic passing from house to house
among the white peoples, and some of us.
That Reverend Rockwell say drink is evil,
and now they done started a Society
for the Promotion of Temperance, and they want
everybody in town to resolve to abstain
entirely from spirituous liquors.
Reverend Rockwell, he say I'm on the road to hell,
ungodly, unhumbled, and incorrigible.
Whatever the hell that mean. And what the hell:
Don't he know I was born and raised in hell?
Excommunicate me from their church?
Don't make me laugh. I never had a place at that table.
My God and me got a understanding:
He keep me supplied with ardent spirit;
I praise Him, fingers crossed behind my back.

Robert B. Shaw (1947)

The poetry of Robert B. Shaw, like the poetry of John Donne, of which Shaw is a scholar, often begins with an observation about everyday objects or events—the chirp of cicadas, the function of bookmarks, climbing a ladder, dawn, an ant in amber. These objects or events are transformed by the poet's acute attention and wry imagination. Dust motes in the afternoon sun become symbols of life's impermanence, a geode teaches us to cherish mystery, and a bait store reminds us of the value of small pleasures. Shaw's poems are governed by tight logic and regular meter, which, combined with a conversational diction, make them feel both polished and off-hand. They are made things and living things at the same time, the result of artifice and spontaneity.

While rarely directly devotional, Shaw's work is nevertheless permeated by a Christian sensibility. In the title poem from his collection *Solving for X*, for example, Shaw observes that the sign, which is also the "monogram of Christ," is notable for its plasticity. It is everywhere and can mean almost anything. Yet, it calls "for our attention from all sides" to something beyond itself—the hope of crossed fingers, the fear of death and destruction in the "sturdy tape bracing each staring window / in the gray lull before the hurricane hits." In another poem, a fallen maple key reminds Shaw of the longing and promise of new life: "It hinges / on going underground, and finding there / hiding inside him what I see I've been / rummaging for myself, the elusive key / offering entry to the sun-crossed air." And in still another poem, "A Geode," an ancient rock is a symbol of Christ and a reminder that what is "of unremarkable appearance" can contain within itself remarkable beauty, which, in turn, can only be perceived by faith.

Shaw studied under Robert Lowell and Robert Fitzgerald. He received his AB from Harvard and PhD from Yale. He is emeritus professor of English at Mount Holyoke College, where he previously served as the Emily Dickinson Professor of English. Author of seven volumes of poetry, including *The Wonder of Seeing Double*, *Solving for X*, and *Aromatics*, as well as a prose study of the poetry of John Donne and George Herbert and a guide to blank verse, Shaw is a winner of the James Boatwright III Prize for Poetry and a recipient of fellowships from the National Endowment for the Arts and the Ingram Merrill Foundation.

THINGS WE WILL NEVER KNOW

What became of Krishna
the blue point Siamese
strayed *circa* Nineteen
Fifty-five in Levittown

Or the box turtle Churchy
lost a few years later
What seduced them away   Where
is Jimmy Hoffa   Judge Crater

What was the name of the dwarf
newsboy we used to buy
Sunday papers from for seven
years until we moved

Who were the Cardinals named
in pectore by the dead Pope
What's in the Fatima letter
Why did Lester leave the Church

Why did his wife leave him
Why didn't she leave him sooner
What made him drink like that
How much did the children know

Who built Stonehenge   Why
Where do the Gypsies come from
Did Cranmer really carry
his wife around in a trunk

Who was it with a smoker's cough
that kept us jerking awake for months
How could walls have been so thin
When did they tear that building down

Who burned down the Reichstag
What is the Great Sphinx watching for
What have we lost for ever when
the shy dream edges away

What do we look like when we sleep
When it's done with who will come
to close our uninquisitive eyes
and make the arrangements needed

Ash Wednesday, Late Afternoon

Dust-motes bustling up—or is it
in, or through—this afternoon's
lazily sloping chute of light
seem intent above all to scatter
havoc along the grand
avenue that irradiates
their antics, unprogressive, up *and* down,
I now see, tracking one or two
only to lose them soon in the lit swarm.
Inflamed with no mere ardor now to rise
but at whatever risk to swing and shine
in these remoter reaches of the sun's decline
they do, in fact, dazzle as they conduct
carnival turns and vaults in bliss above
their stunned confederates thickening on the carpet—
the fatal plain to which they too
will settle. Don't they know it? When they do,
they will have lost their audience, hung
in cooling air, the sun's last ladder rung
tweaked from beneath them, finding this to be
an unappreciative arena where
the act winds down after the spotlight's moved.
Their ultimate stunts, in graying vacancy,
are dartings we can take only on trust,
picturing that deserted turbulence
dimly subsiding, mating dust to dust.

A GEODE
for Peter Olenchuk

What started out a glob of molten mud
hawked up by some Brazilian volcano
back in the Pleistocene is now a rock
of unremarkable appearance, brown
as ordinary mud and baseball-size.
Picking it up produces the surprise:
besides a pleasant heftiness, a sound
of sloshing can be noticed. Vapors caught
within its cooling crust were liquified,
and linger still: a million-year-old vintage.
Although one might recall the once ubiquitous
snowstorm-in-a-glass-globe paperweights,
this offers us no view inside to gauge
the wild weather a shake or two incites.
Turbulence masked by hard opacity. . . .
If we could, which would we rather see?
Age-old distillate, infant tears of the earth,
or gem-like crystal of the inner walls
harboring them like some fair reliquary?
To see the one we'd have to spill the other.
Better to keep it homely and intact,
a witness to the worth of hiddenness,
which, in regard to our own kind, we call
reticence, and in terms of higher things,
mystery. Let the elixir drench unseen
the facets that enshrine it, world without end.

DEC. 23

He's finished tacking up the Christmas garland
so it arrays the Parish Hall at one end,
loops of glistering tinsel off a rafter.
Nagged by Sunday School teachers, none of whom
could reach to do it, he brought up his ladder
and hammered through their bicker of suggestions
to pin the swags the way he damn well wanted.
Under this job tomorrow an eight-year-old boy,
a seven-year-old girl will cradle
a large, diapered baby doll between them,
while shepherds of the same age, some of them
notorious brats, stand burlap-clad with canes,
lording it over younger ones on all fours
and wrapped in artificial fleece, no lines
to learn, just lots of docile, brutish kneeling.
It's like this every year, the eve of the Eve;
hung up, the silvery furbelow now seems
to emphasize the bareness of the space
beneath it, wintry Bethlehem of worn
linoleum facing ranks of metal chairs
he set up once the ladies left him to it.
It will have to do. Only the garland
and the direction of the gathered chairs
will make this patch of floor into a stage.
Parents, onlookers will watch as children
pretend to be parents and onlookers
in a receding time, a distant place.
Tired, he folds his ladder, bumps it down
to stow it in the basement, takes a look
at the oil burner, hearing once again
that ticking noise he doesn't like. Upstairs,
although he never aimed to make a still life,
he's done just that in absentmindedness
on a west windowsill. But no one's here
(is it too early or is it too late?)
to watch the things glint when the white spear

of sunlight touches them: his laid-aside
claw hammer and a handful of long nails.
Instruments of the Passion. Tools of somebody's trade.

PILGRIMS

White as a baby's tooth, the little church
pokes up from the apostate wilderness
of onetime farms gone back to scrubby woods.
Everything's cradled snug in sabbath peace
as we approach, but suddenly, as if
we'd tripped a wire, there is a soft moan
and wheeze set off inside—the balky organ—
and then the singing, adamant and loud,
vehement exhalations taking heart
from heaving all together, as though one
ultimate heave could raise the clapboard box
off its foundation, scooting it to heaven
on a self-generated gust of rapture.
Choir practice, probably, this being
Saturday afternoon. Pent in their resonant
unornamented boards, the choir must
comprise a great part of the congregation,
so dollhouse-like the building is. The hymn
trumpets a challenge to the tuckered-out
surrounding countryside to the effect of
Hear and be saved—which is, of course, beyond
its compass, sunk in drought-depleted stupor.
Casual, sweating passersby like us
may not intend to pay much greater heed;
but a few words do pelt us, slipping through
the chuffed accompaniment, the weighty drone.
Something about "O Savior, when we die
(de-dum, de-dum) thy dwelling place on high."
Words are prone to blur in the fervent yearning
broadcast from the louvered bottom panes
of those embattled-looking pointy windows.

Haunting the air, it cannot stir the dust
even as much as we do, shuffling past.
While we're still in earshot, the sound dies.
Rehearsal must be over. Yes, they're coming
out now, and I count them, half a dozen
women and four men. They clamber into
a decommissioned school bus, painted blue,
which we now see was parked around in back.
And we, wrapped in heat and resumed silence,
what are we out here looking for today?
We keep on going, down to the dry creek
to hunt for arrowheads. It's said to be
the place for this, but after a hot hour
of scrabbling through the pebble beds we find
exactly two, a flint for each of us.
Chipped to a razor-edge, they're tapered to
carpenter-gothic points much like the windows
out of which poured the ministry of song.
Which are the points that nick the soul more keenly—
those of the lost or those of the lingering tribe?

Kathleen Norris (1947)

Kathleen Norris was born in 1947 in Washington, D.C., and is a poet and memoirist perhaps best known for her nonfiction books *Dakota: A Spiritual Geography*, which received a *New York Times* Notable Book Citation, *The Cloister Walk*, and *Amazing Grace*, all of which constitute a sort of spiritual autobiography. In addition to these and five other nonfiction books, she is the author of five volumes of poetry and a regular contributor for *The Christian Century* and other magazines. Having grown up largely in Hawaii, she has made her home there again after many years in South Dakota, the backdrop for much of her work.

A married Protestant who became an oblate of a Catholic Benedictine monastery, Norris writes across personal and religious divides, illuminating the value of monastic celibacy, for example, as a figure for universal human experiences of sacrifice and self-giving which become, paradoxically, sources of joy. This insight, which recognizes the ways that the practices, structures, and truths of a particular mode of religious life resonate through *all* life, permeates Norris's body of poetic work as well. Consider her poem "Ascension," in which Christ's ascension into heaven—signaled by the title and epigraph, from the first chapter of the Acts of the Apostles, but not otherwise made explicit in the poem—is juxtaposed with forces in the material world. The first stanza concerns the weather: gusts and updrafts of "excited air" imparting "the feeling that one might ascend / . . . rising like a trumpet note." The second, paradoxically, takes up the onset of childbirth. "And it wasn't just my sister's water breaking, / her crying out, / the downward draw of blood and bone." In stanza three the earth is thrusting up its own new life, even as the laboring mother is bearing down. Stanza to stanza, this is a poem of juxtapositions, life forces pulling up or pulling down, culminating in a birth. The child leaves the mother's body to enter a new, separate existence: "beginning the long goodbye." Both the Ascension itself—the risen Christ's birth into heaven, that "long goodbye"—and the spring day at the end of Eastertide which memorializes it, frame, integrate, and grant larger meaning to all these disparate earthly movements and events, even as Christ, as Saint Paul has it in his letter to the Colossians, "holds all creation together in himself."

Paradox and juxtaposition characterize Norris's work, the dissonance at the heart of mystery. "A Prayer to Eve" offers our First Mother as a patron saint—"mother of fictions"—as if what had arisen from the Fall was simultaneously the happy fault of art and learning, the sad critical distance of self-knowledge, and the weary journey of exile. Like the monks praying the Mass in the church, such poems as "The Sky Is Full of Blue, and Full of the Mind of God" are "playing at a serious game." Their game, like the monks', is that of speaking what ultimately cannot be said, of finding its substance, which the monks find in the Eucharist, in the sky, in the wind, in a singer's reaching voice, all of which her speaker knows as holy. "I stood rooted to the spot," says the speaker in "Little Girls in Church," "and looked up, and believed." Though the belief of that moment "didn't last," still this is the stance of these poems: rooted to some spot in the intimate, physical, fleeting world, and in that moment, like the marveling men of Galilee, looking up.

PRAYER TO EVE

Mother of fictions
and of irony,
help us to laugh.

Mother of science
and the critical method,
keep us humble.

Muse of listeners,
hope of interpreters,
inspire us to act.

Bless our metaphors,
that we might eat them.

Help us to know, Eve,
the one thing we must do.

Come with us, muse of exile,
mother of the road.

LITTLE GIRLS IN CHURCH

1.

I've made friends
with a five-year-old
Presbyterian. She tugs at her lace collar,
I sympathize. We're both bored.
I give her a pencil;
she draws the moon,
grass, stars,
and I name them for her,
printing in large letters.
The church bulletin
begins to fill.
Carefully she prints her name—KATHY—
and hands it back.

Just last week,
in New York City, the Orthodox liturgy
was typically intimate,
casual. An old woman greeted the icons
one by one,
and fell asleep
during the Great Litany.
People went in and out
to smoke cigarettes and chat on the steps.

A girl with long brown braids
was led to the icons
by her mother. They kissed each one,
and the girl made a confession
to the youngest priest. I longed to hear it,
to know her name.

2.

I worry for the girls.
I once had braids,
and wore lace that made me suffer.
I had not yet done the things

that would need forgiving.
Church was for singing, and so I sang.
I received a Bible, stars
for all the verses;
I turned and ran.

The music brought me back
from time to time,
singing hymns
in the great breathing body
of a congregation.
And once in Paris, as
I stepped into Notre Dame
to get out of the rain,
the organist began to play:
I stood rooted to the spot,
looked up, and believed.

It didn't last.
Dear girls, my friends,
may you find great love
within you, starlike
and wild, as wide as grass,
solemn as the moon.
I will pray for you, if I can.

THE SKY IS FULL OF BLUE, AND FULL OF THE MIND OF GOD

a girl wrote once
in winter, in a school
at Minot Air Force Base.
A girl tall for her age,
with cornrows and a shy, gap-toothed smile.
She was lonely in North Dakota,
for God, for trees,
warm weather, the soft cadences of Louisiana.

I think of her,
as the sky stretches tight all around.
I'm at the Conoco on I-94, waiting for the eastbound bus.
Mass is not over; the towers of the monastery
give no sign
that deep in the church
men in robes and chasubles
are playing at a serious game.

I feel like dancing on this
wooden porch: "Gotta get to you, baby,
been runnin' all over town."
The jukebox is wired to be heard outside
and I dance to keep warm,
my breath carried white on the breeze.

The sky stretches tight, a mandorla of cloud
around the sun. And now
Roy Orbison reaches for the stratosphere:
something about a blue angel.
It is the Sanctus; I know it; I'm ready.

Ascension

Why do you stand looking up at the skies?
    —Acts 1:11

It wasn't just wind, chasing
thin gunmetal clouds
across the loud sky;
it wasn't the feeling that one might ascend
on that excited air,
rising like a trumpet note.

And it wasn't just my sister's water breaking,
her crying out,
the downward draw of blood and bone . . .

It was all of that,
the mud and new grass

pushing up through melting snow,
the lilac in bud
by my front door, bent low
by last week's ice storm.

Now the new mother, that leaky vessel,
begins to nurse her child,
beginning the long good-bye.

William Baer (1948)

Born in 1948 in Geneva, New York, William Baer is perhaps best known for his role in the New Formalist Movement in contemporary American poetry. As founding editor of *The Formalist* poetry journal, contributing editor for the literary magazine *Measure,* and founding director of both the Richard Wilbur Award for book-length poetry manuscripts and the Howard Nemerov Sonnet Award, Baer has long been an advocate for contemporary poets writing metrical verse, in a literary landscape which had habituated itself to hostility toward such poetry. In his tenure as poetry editor for the Catholic magazine *Crisis,* Baer was further instrumental in establishing a platform for poets of faith, specifically, within the larger circle of New Formalism. This overlap of "formalist poet" with "poet of faith" is hardly accidental; in Baer's view, as in the view of many formalist poets who are Christians, the order which poetic form, particularly meter, imposes on language both echoes and declares itself to be an element in God's ordering of the created world. This vision of order extends as well to Baer's work as a fiction writer preoccupied with the detective story, whose narrative arc is inscribed within the bounds of a just universe.

Baer is a contemporary master of the sonnet, that fourteen-line rhyming form made famous by Petrarch in fourteenth-century Italy, and handed from Italian into English by way of the sixteenth-century diplomat and poet Sir Thomas Wyatt. His 2011 collection, *Psalter: A Sequence of Catholic Sonnets,* meditates on the sweeping narrative of salvation—"God's saving acts in history"—through the Old and New Testaments by means of the sonnet, a form particularly suited, in its rhetorical structure, to contemplation and interior argument. Even when writing in other forms, including invented forms, Baer remains in conversation with the sonnet tradition, as in his 1997 debut collection, *The Unfortunates,* which received the inaugural T. S. Eliot Poetry Prize from Truman State University Press. This sequence's sixteen-line poems, each a double octave focused, like a sort of *Spoon River Noir,* on the story of an "unfortunate" person, wind up and resolve themselves as Petrarchan sonnets do in the move from octet to sestet. In this collection, however, Baer employs that action in the service of narrative, rather than the lyric argumentation conventionally associated with the sonnet form. With this first book, he established himself as an artist who affirms literary tradition as a living, dynamic terrain, whose boundaries the poet never rejects but seeks to expand.

In addition to his six books of poetry, William Baer is also the author of a book of sonnets translated from the Portuguese, two poetry anthologies, and a textbook, *Writing Metrical Poetry.* A fiction writer as well as a poet, he has written two crime novels and two collections of short stories. He is also a gifted and prolific literary and artistic interviewer, who has published multiple collected "conversations," including *Thirteen on Form: Conversations with Poets* and books of interviews with the poet Derek

Walcott and the film director Elia Kazan. A film critic and a playwright, Baer has written a range of historical dramas and comedies, as well as a musical adaptation of Jane Austen's *Persuasion*. Besides the T. S. Eliot Poetry Prize for *The Unfortunates*, he has received the X. J. Kennedy Poetry Prize, the Jack Nicholson Screenwriting Award, the James H. Wilson Playwriting Award, the New Works of Merit Playwriting Award, and the AACT NewPlayFest Award for 2015. He is also the recipient of an N.E.A. Creative Writing Fellowship in Fiction and a Guggenheim Fellowship, and has held the Melvin M. Peterson Chair in Literature at the University of Evansville.

SNAKE

Genesis 3:5

Yes, you have a lovely garden here,
with flowers, fields and fruits, lakes and streams,
beneath a Tree of Life, with nothing to fear,
in a paradise of pleasure, a place of dreams.
And, yes, you have each other's trust and love,
naked, as if one flesh, chaste and free;
and, yes, you have dominion, over and above,
everything as far as the eye can see.
And yet, you lack a certain acuity,
a comprehension of all that lies within,
of good, of evil, of ambiguity,
of death, and of the leprosy of sin.
Become as gods, transform to something new;
put hiss in your voice and fork your tongue in two.

ADAM

Genesis 4:8

Of course, he'd seen this "thing" before, but never
like this. After Eden, he'd found a swan
lying motionless and silent forever,
rotting, irretrievable, and gone.
But now it's his boy, the brother of Cain,
the shepherd son, the kind and faithful friend
of He-Who-Is, lying quiet and slain:
finished, futureless, at the end of his end.
Once, Adam had named the names, and named his own
two sons, and named this curse, which nullifies
and terminates, as "death." But he who'd known
the awesome power of God looked to the skies,
knowing, without a doubt, though nothing was said,
his God both could and would undo the dead.

THEOTOKOS

Luke 1:38

Before eternity, in timeless space,
in timelessness, in time before all-time,
the mind of God, with enigmatic grace,
conceived that Panagia, the paradigm,
goal of generative history,
the masterpiece, of whom God said
that she and her seed, that fathomless mystery,
would crush the serpent's bloody head.
Who seemed an obscure Jewish girl until
that moment-of-moments when she would say:
"Fiat," the handmaid of her Father's will,
to consummate eternity, then pray
humbly accepting she-knows-not-what,
singing her silent Magnificat.

ETHIOPIAN

Acts 8:31

In the Gaza desert, in the heat of the day,
he craved the only truth that could set him free.
Sitting in his chariot, he puzzled away,
struggling with Isaiah fifty:three.
Yes, even one well-tutored in his youth,
even the mighty minister of the Queen,
could only wrestle with the scriptural truth,
which seemed mysterious and serpentine.
Then Philip, the "anointed," approached and said,
"Can you understand what you're reading now?"
but the humble magistrate just shook his head.
"Not unless someone shows me how."
So Philip explained, beneath the Gaza skies,
and the truths of the world opened before their eyes.

Jay Parini (1948)

Jay Parini was born in Pittston, Pennsylvania, and raised in Scranton. He has a BA from Lafayette College and a PhD from the University of St. Andrews in Scotland. He is the author of six books of poetry, including *Town Life*, *The Art of Subtraction*, and *New and Collected Poems, 1975-2015*, which collects his best work over the past forty years. His novels include *Benjamin's Crossing* and *The Passages of H. M.*, among others, and he is the author of several works of nonfiction, including biographies of Robert Frost, William Faulkner, Jesus, and Gore Vidal. He is currently the D. E. Axinn Professor of English and Creative Writing at Middlebury College and a former fellow of both the Institute for Advanced Studies at the University of London and Christ Church at Oxford University.

In a 2008 interview with Mitch Wertlieb for Vermont Public Radio, Parini remarked that poetry is "language that conducts us towards the center of our experience as human beings." Experiential is one way to think about Parini's poetry. He often attempts to capture a moment of feeling in his work, which functions as each poem's unifying device. With the lyrical "I" at the center, his poems move from situational observation to insight in a way that can be similar to both Robert Frost and Adrienne Rich. "There is always movement, muttering, / in flight to wisdom, / which cannot be fixed," Parini writes in "The Grammar of Affection," which is included in this volume. "The kingdom / comes but gradually," he continues, "breaking word by wing or day by dream."

So, too, with Parini's poetry, which possesses both a distinct movement towards wisdom but also an awareness of the halting and incomplete nature of that movement. "Sad," Parini writes in "The Prophets," "how few words / are true enough to matter." Even words that are true enough do not always matter in the way we might have hoped. "In the chapel dark," Parini writes in "At the Ruined Monastery," "I'm trying to make out a worn inscription / on a wind-smudged altar, / but the Latin hieroglyphs have lost their /edge." Yet, where other poets might see this as a reason to despair, Parini, a tentative optimist, sees an occasion to exercise faith in a God who speaks and hears and who, by virtue of being the eternal Word, salvages language's power. Parini concludes "At the Ruined Monastery" with a prayer: "Remember me, *Signore*, / who has not yet learned to read your hand, / its alphabet of buzz and drip and flutter." This is not a dead language the poet is referring to but a living one—one that buzzes and flutters.

AT THE RUINED MONASTERY IN AMALFI
for Charles Wright

On a hill, approaching Easter,
well above the sea's bland repetitions
of the same old story
and the town's impenitent composure,
I survey old grounds.

The fire-winged gulls ungulf the tower.
Lesser grackles, nuns and tourists,
scatter on the grass.

The brandy-colored light of afternoon
seeps through the stonework;
creeping flowers buzz and flutter
in the limestone cracks.

Wisteria-chocked loggias drip with sun.

A honeycomb of cells absorbs the absence
it has learned to savor;
court and cloister close on silence,
the auroral prayers long since burned off
like morning fog.

The business of eternity goes on behind our
backs.

In the chapel dark,
I'm trying to make out a worn inscription
on a wind-smudged altar,
but the Latin hieroglyphs have lost their
edge.

Remember me, *Signore*,
who has not yet learned to read your hand,
its alphabet of buzz and drip and flutter.

THE GRAMMAR OF AFFECTION

Without syntax there is no immortality,
says my friend,
who has counted beads along a string
and understood that time is
water in a brook
or words in passage,
caravans amid the whitest dunes,
a team of horses in the mountain trace.

There is always movement, muttering,
in flight to wisdom,
which cannot be fixed. The kingdom
comes but gradually,
breaking word by wing or day by dream.

We proceed on insufficient knowledge,
trusting in what comes, in what comes down
in winding corridors,
in clamorous big rooms,
above a gorge on windy cliffs.

In places where discovered sounds make sense,
where subjects run through verbs
to matter in the end, a natural completion
in the holy object of affections
as our sentence circles round again:

This grammar holds us, makes us shine.

BLESSINGS

Blessings for these things:
the dandelion greens I picked in summer
and would douse with vinegar and oil
at grandma's little house in Pennsylvania,
near the river. Or the small potatoes
she would spade to boil and butter,
which I ate like fruit with greasy fingers.

Blessings for my friend, thirteen
that summer when we prayed by diving from a cliff
on Sunday mornings in the church
of mud and pebbles, foam and moss.
I will not forget the fizz and tingle,
sunning in wet skin on flat, cool rocks,
so drenched in summer.

And for you, my love, blessings
for the times we lay so naked in a bed
without the sense of turbulence or tides.
I could just believe the softness of our skin,
those sheets like clouds,
how when the sunlight turned to roses,
neither of us dared to move or breathe.

Blessings on these things and more:
the rivers and the houses full of light,
the bitter weeds that taste like sun,
dirt-sweetened spuds,
the hard bright pebbles, spongy mosses,
lifting of our bodies into whiffs of cloud,
all sleep-warm pillows in the break of dawn.

David Middleton (1949)

"To render such grim dignity divine." This line, which ends David Middleton's poem "Man With a Hoe," on a painting by Jean-François Millet, points not only to Millet's artistic project, but to Middleton's own. "Dignity" is an apt phrase for the character of Middleton's poems, rooted in the bayou landscapes of his native Louisiana, with its turbulent history and weathers, but also in personal history, filled with griefs and losses, gifts and quiet joys. The poet and novelist Fred Chappell has characterized Middleton's poetry as "stately": a "rare quality . . . achieved through technical mastery, devote labor, judicious sympathy, and loving contemplation." Certainly there is devotion in Middleton's exacting attention to the formal details of rhyme and meter, which order the wildernesses of physical and interior landscapes—or to put it more precisely, *discern* existing order, intrinsic dignity, in those wildernesses, to articulate that dignity in ordered language.

Middleton's poems, and his own sense of himself as poet, ground themselves in a world which, though fallen and forgetful, remains bounded, shaped, and articulated by tradition. His poem "Ordinations" juxtaposes a young man's reception of Anglican Holy Orders at the hands of his bishop, in apostolic succession, with the poet's own sense of vocation which springs from its own apostolic succession. In the poet's case, the succession derives from an even more ancient origin than Christian ordination does. If the priest operates, by virtue of his ordination, *in persona Christi,* then the poet, as Middleton himself has suggested in an essay entitled "The Striking of the Lyre: Demodokos in Modernity," functions in the person of Homer's bard Demodokos, a figure briefly but potently encountered by Odysseus in his wanderings. Odysseus, disguised, overhears Demodokos singing to his lyre of the fall of Troy. The bard's song is Odysseus's own story, as the wanderer perceives in a flash of self-recognition that moves him to weep. The potency of this encounter lies in the power of the song itself to awaken Odysseus, who has just escaped Kalypso's amnesiac enchantments, to the full memory of his humanity and his place in the world: "poetry's shattering revelation of who he is." As Middleton suggests, poetry's ultimate ambition is to restore us to ourselves, in the wholeness of the *Imago Dei:* "to render such grim dignity divine." It is in this apostolic succession that the poet is ordained, to this vocation and charism of restoration.

Born in Shreveport, Louisiana, in 1949, David Middleton taught for many years at Nicholls State University in Thibodeaux, Louisiana, serving as Professor of English, Poet-in-Residence, and head of the Department of Languages and Literature. His honors in academic life have included his appointment as Distinguished Service Professor and Alcee Fortier Distinguished Professor. His books of poetry include *The Burning Fields, As Far as Light Remains, Beyond the Chandeleurs, The Habitual Peacefulness of Gruchy,* and *The Fiddler of Driskill Hill.* In 2006 he received the Allen Tate Award from the *Sewanee Review,* where he has been a longtime frequent contributor, for a poem published the previous year, and the State of Louisiana Governor's Award for Outstanding Professional Artist. He has served as poetry editor for *Anglican Theological Review, The Classical Outlook,* and *Modern Age.*

MAN WITH A HOE
ca. 1863

He leans on the short handle, knotted oak,
Its flat blade pressed on brambled clay and stone.
A boulder shoulders thorns up from the soil
While oxen plow a far-off pastoral farm

Whose stubble-fires smoke white toward skies in haze.
He dominates the land as serf and lord,
The subject monarch of his stark domain,
His thistle-crown root-bound in freehold earth.

Not fallen from some paradise whose crops
Turned golden while he plucked a harp's ripe strings,
He'd come down long hard centuries the same,
Man's bent-back state no revolutions change.

Millet made no more gestures after this
But concentrated on technique alone,
Placing his faith in color, shape, and line
To render such grim dignity divine.

LOUISIANA PASSAGE: THE WHIPPOORWILL
for Jack Wise

A night or two in April, then no more
They call in latest twilight from the skies,
Migrants who fly between the stars and foam
Now come to this hard ground where dark abides.
And when the moon illumines each chill bloom
Of dandelion and violet and flag
Still trembling in a latent winter gloom,
The birds sing their own name so clean and clear—
Whip-poor-will, whip-poor-will, whip-poor-will—then
Swooping to scoop up insects on the wing,
Mayflies and ladybugs in those wide mouths,
They feed and fly away to nesting-grounds

Remote from those the Caddo[28] once had known
Deep in the virgin stands of silent pine.

And yet in gold October they return
Ghostly over the uplands' folded wolds,
Riding the ancient flyway as they climb
Into a dawn where centuries ago
Their ancestors had crossed without a cry
Green kingdoms of the oak and tupelo
Unbroken from Ozarks to the coast.
And pausing there upon the last chenier,
Made voiceless as they gaze beyond the Gulf
Toward some catholic South their flight implies,
They listen with intent for one who calls
Each creature in the language of its name,
And when they hear they pass through silent skies
Toward Adam and the earthly paradise.

THE SUNDAY SCHOOL LESSON
north Louisiana

The room was full of thirteen-year-old boys
Unhappily constrained by polished shoes,
Bow ties, oiled hair, and orders against all noise,
And one eternal hour of Good News.

I joined the class each summer in July
When visiting my kin in that small town,
Lazing away the weeks till by and by
The signs of autumn brought my parents down.

Distracted like the rest, I too was bored,
Though not a friend who shared the cycling year's
High rites of church, school, farm, and sports that stored
A common mind with common loves and fears.

28 The Caddo: a confederation of Native American tribes, part of the larger mound-building
Mississippian culture of the Southeast, whose territory, before their nineteenth-century removal
to reservations, covered areas of Louisiana, Texas, Oklahoma, and Arkansas.

Long-legged and ungainly in my chair
I'd lean on the shoved-up window while the fan
Would spin a weightless haze of heated air
Around the sullen room as class began.

Jack Hopkins was our teacher, though I doubt
He ever saw himself as any more
Than someone who could see an hour out
With tall tales of his catch the night before.

I'd watch his bulbous nose and long-drawn face
Both reddened in a steady heart's decline
As once more he would tell, with skill and grace,
How to land nine-pound bass with a two-pound line.

One day, though, he seemed different, hardly there
Gazing over the graves with restless eyes
Searching for something distant and yet near
Unfixable in cloudless summer skies.

At last, he slowly read, then half-recited
In a strong drawl that measured out King James
Those passages in Matthew where affrighted
Disciples cried to Jesus as He came

Walking across night's foam upon the water
To grasp weakening Peter who'd looked down
Distracted by the winds that made him totter,
Now mastered by the fear that he would drown.

Fumbling with his glasses, Mr. Jack then tried
With chuckles and an animated glance
Around a room from which all sound had died
To end the solemn calm and his own trance.

Those verses always moved him, he confessed,
Because of that strange evening on the lake
When a sudden storm caught him and he pressed
Against its wind to reach a cypress brake.

Perhaps it was the play of dark and light
Or just his tiredness vivified with fear
And yet he swore that at the torrent's height
He saw the Christ by lightning drawing near.

With that the lesson ended and the class
Rose awkwardly one by one and left the room
Embarrassed, even scared to have to pass
This man who'd gazed beyond the body's doom.

And though time brought him soon to what he saw,
It took me over thirty years to know
How soul's redeemed by wonder, lost in awe
Before those depths through which I still must go

With doubt and faith like Peter on the sea,
Sinking in fear and chaos of the foam,
Yet looking up toward one who has to be
There before the winds to take us home.

Self-Examination: Reflections in a Mirror

Time once again for my six-months' exam
I stand before a mirror to assess
This aging body's state, each troubling sign
I'll need to show my doctor—lumps or moles,
Tingling or numbness, belly fat or sores,
Heart palpitations, rashes, there with things
Beyond all cure, that sag or fall away.
But then I see what mirrored eyes now say,
Those portals of the soul where sheer light sings
Till mind will discipline while love implores
The flesh to give itself to old controls
So virtue every sin might soon confine
Till soul is more and more, the body less
And who I should have been is what I am.

EPIPHANY IN LENT

The last parade has finished in the dusk
And all the floats come back through Thibodaux
From downtown to the college parking lot.
The king and queen and princesses have gone
To dance at fancy balls till midnight brings
This dark night of the liver to its end.
Like witches, ghosts, and trolls at Halloween
Banished on All Saints Day, these costumed gods—
Bacchus, Venus, Mars—now vanish into ash.
The power lines and trees are hung with beads
A few of which will be there in July,
Dry, cracked, and bleached through Caesar's summer reign.
The air still smells of beer and barbecue—
Elements bodies bless at Mardi Gras—
And diehard revelers head to bayou bars
While I, with curtains drawn, remain apart
As I have done for more than forty years
Both from the Protestant north and Catholic south,
Louisiana's European divide:
My '50s Shreveport with its endless Lent
Of guilt and blue laws regnant in between
The red-light streets and "game" ships on the Red
And Thibodaux's high feasts of flesh and blood
Lashed to a passionate abstinence,
Those twin sad aftermaths of Christendom.
And there I stay, secluded with the muse,
Heeding the poet's calling to withdraw
So that he can more fully come to be
The alien celebrator of his home
Shown in the heartfelt psalms his mind refines,
The native foreigner who carries on
As crafter of the wordsmith's mysteries
Forging with fire and sweat his image-beads
Like throws that hang on lines like lines of poems
Or pollen riming spring's Bienville hills,
Fat Tuesday, thin Ash Wednesday, hymned as one.

ORDINATIONS

priest, poet

"Receive this Bible as a sign . . ." The Book of Common Prayer, 534

Younger than I by nearly forty years,
He stands for examination, then kneels,
The bishop laying hands upon the head
Of one who prays for strength to rise again,
Holding on tight to a Bible, the gift
A bishop gives to all whom God has called
To preach the Word and offer bread and wine.

Here in the pews, near three score years and ten,
I see myself—and not—in that young man,
For I was also called, ordained, my gift
Not given by a bishop but a voice
That left me with the silence of the page
And language from a common lexicon,
The Holy Spirit blessing *grape* and *grain.*

Dana Gioia (1950)

Dana Gioia was born in 1950 in Los Angeles and grew up in Hawthorne, a working-class suburb just a few miles from the Los Angeles International Airport. His mother was Mexican American. His father's family was from Sicily. Catholicism permeated his early life. He attended St. Joseph's Catholic School and Junipero Serra High School, which was run by French Marianists who drilled students in Latin, theology, Augustine, and Aquinas. "Growing up in a Latin community of Sicilians and Mexicans," Gioia told Robert McPhillips in 1992, "one didn't feel the Roman Catholic Church as an abstraction. It was a living culture." Gioia went to Stanford after high school, took an MA in Comparative Literature at Harvard, where he studied under Elizabeth Bishop and Robert Fitzgerald, and returned to Stanford for an MBA. He worked for many years as a vice president at General Foods and served as the chairman of the National Endowment for the Arts from 2003 to 2009.

Gioia's great interests as a poet are the vicissitudes of love, the mystery of ordinary things, the power and limits of language, and the redemptive nature of suffering. In his poem "Words," Gioia writes: "The world does not need words," pushing back against the grandiose theory of the artist as a maker of reality. Rather, it "articulates itself / in sunlight, leaves, and shadows." Yet, "the stones remain less real to those who cannot / name them." The task of the poet is to find a language to speak of what is present and obscure, ubiquitous and unobserved, axiomatic and paradoxical, mundane and mysterious. This approach has produced poems of unusual power and wisdom. "Beware of things in duplicate," Gioia writes in an eponymous poem, "a set of knives, the cufflinks in a drawer":

These are the moments to beware
when here this nothing so familiar
or so close that it cannot betray you:
a twin, an extra key, an echo,
your own reflection in the glass.

Throughout his work, Gioia shows that we see but fail to observe; we trust, but trust the wrong thing. We love what should be hated, and live for what is dead. This is why Gioia writes in "Prayer at Winter Solstice": "Blessed is the road that keeps us homeless. / Blessed is the mountain that blocks our way." Suffering is a form of grace, redirecting our wayward affections and paths towards a good we would not otherwise choose. Gioia suggests in "The Burning Ladder" and "Prophecy" that suffering is a surer path to holiness—if anything can be said to be sure in this world—than a vision or religious experience. After all, what is a vision other than a form of listening, and what is listening other than a turning away from oneself, which can only be learned through suffering.

Gioia is not all work and no play, however. Included in the selections in this volume are "The Archbishop," a lighthearted skewering of a literary critic figured as an archbishop who has lost sight of his calling, and the humorous but serious "Seven Deadly Sins."

Poetry that doesn't please is no poetry at all, and what often please in poetry are music and storytelling. "Art craves teleology," Gioia has observed, and poetry is no exception. His work is noteworthy for its narrative drive, as well as for its formal and topical range. He is at home in meter and free verse and can turn from a lament on the plight of beautiful movie stars to a meditation on the work of Søren Kierkegaard.

Gioia has published five volumes of poetry, six volumes of criticism, and several anthologies. He wrote the libretto for *Nosferatu* and has had several poems set to music. He is a National Book Critics Circle Award finalist and a winner of the American Book Award. Among his many awards are the John Ciardi Award for Lifetime Achievement in Poetry, The Presidential Citizens Medal, the University of Notre Dame's Laetare Medal, the Aiken Taylor Award for Lifetime Achievement in American Poetry, and the Denise Levertov Award. He taught for many years at the University of Southern California, where he was the Judge Widney Professor of Poetry and Public Culture, and has served as the Poet Laureate of California since 2015.

THE BURNING LADDER

Jacob
never climbed the ladder
burning in his dream. Sleep
pressed him like a stone
in the dust,
and when
he should have risen
like a flame to join
that choir, he was sick
of travelling,
and closed
his eyes to the Seraphim
ascending, unconscious
of the impossible distances
between their steps,
missed
them mount the brilliant
ladder, slowly disappearing
into the scattered light
between the stars,
slept

through it all, a stone
upon a stone pillow,
shivering, Gravity
always greater than desire.

PRAYER

Echo of the clocktower, footstep
in the alleyway, sweep
of the wind sifting the leaves.

Jeweller of the spiderweb, connoisseur
of autumn's opulence, blade of lightning
harvesting the sky.

Keeper of the small gate, choreographer
of entrances and exits, midnight
whisper traveling the wires.

Seducer, healer, deity or thief,
I will see you soon enough—
in the shadow of the rainfall,

in the brief violet darkening a sunset—
but until then I pray watch over him
as a mountain guards its covert ore

and the harsh falcon its flightless young.

THE LITANY

This is a litany of lost things,
a canon of possessions dispossessed,
a photograph, an old address, a key.
It is a list of words to memorize
or to forget—of *amo, amas, amat,*[29]
the conjugations of a dead tongue
in which the final sentence has been spoken.

29 Latin conjugations of the verb *love*—"I love, you love, he/she/it loves."

This is the liturgy of rain,
falling on mountain, field, and ocean—
indifferent, anonymous, complete—
of water infinitesimally slow,
sifting through rock, pooling in darkness,
gathering in springs, then rising without our agency,
only to dissolve in mist or cloud or dew.

This is a prayer to unbelief,
to candles guttering and darkness undivided,
to incense drifting into emptiness.
It is the smile of a stone Madonna
and the silent fury of the consecrated wine,
a benediction on the death of a young god,
brave and beautiful, rotting on a tree.

This is a litany to earth and ashes,
to the dust of roads and vacant rooms,
to the fine silt circling in a shaft of sun,
settling indifferently on books and beds.
This is a prayer to praise what we become,
"Dust thou art, to dust thou shalt return."
Savor its taste—the bitterness of earth and ashes.

This is a prayer, inchoate and unfinished,
for you, my love, my loss, my lesion,
a rosary of words to count out time's
illusions, all the minutes, hours, days
the calendar compounds as if the past
existed somewhere—like an inheritance
still waiting to be claimed.

Until at last it is our litany, *mon vieux*,[30]
my reader, my voyeur, as if the mist
steaming from the gorge, this pure paradox,
the shattered river rising as it falls—
splintering the light, swirling it skyward,
neither transparent nor opaque but luminous,
even as it vanishes—were not our life.

30 French expression meaning "old friend."

THE ANGEL WITH THE BROKEN WING

I am the Angel with the Broken Wing,
The one large statue in this quiet room.
The staff finds me too fierce, and so they shut
Faith's ardor in this air-conditioned tomb.

The docents praise my elegant design
Above the chatter of the gallery.
Perhaps I am a masterpiece of sorts—
The perfect emblem of futility.

Mendoza carved me for a country church.
(His name's forgotten now except by me.)
I stood beside a gilded altar where
The hopeless offered God their misery.

I heard their women whispering at my feet—
Prayers for the lost, the dying, and the dead.
Their candles stretched my shadow up the wall,
And I became the hunger that they fed.

I broke my left wing in the Revolution
(Even a saint can savor irony)
When troops were sent to vandalize the chapel.
They hit me once—almost apologetically.

For even the godless feel something in a church,
A twinge of hope, fear? Who knows what it is?
A trembling unaccounted by their laws,
An ancient memory they can't dismiss.

There are so many things I must tell God!
The howling of the damned can't reach so high.
But I stand like a dead thing nailed to a perch,
A crippled saint against a painted sky.

PROPHECY

Sometimes a child will stare out of a window
for a moment or an hour—deciphering
the future from a dusky summer sky.

Does he imagine that some wisp of cloud
reveals the signature of things to come?
Or that the world's a book we learn to translate?

And sometimes a girl stands naked by a mirror
imagining beauty in a stranger's eyes
finding a place where fear leads to desire.

For what is prophecy but the first inkling
of what we ourselves must call into being?
The call need not be large. No voice in thunder.

It's not so much what's spoken as what's heard—
and recognized, of course. The gift is listening
and hearing what is only meant for you.

Life has its mysteries, annunciations,
and some must wear a crown of thorns. I found
my Via Dolorosa in your love.

And sometimes we proceed by prophecy,
or not at all—even if only to know
what destiny requires us to renounce.

O Lord of indirection and ellipses,
ignore our prayers. Deliver us from distraction.
Slow our heartbeat to a cricket's call.

In the green torpor of the afternoon,
bless us with ennui and quietude.
And grant us only what we fear, so that

Underneath the murmur of the wasp
we hear the dry grass bending in the wind
and the spider's silken whisper from its web.

Prayer at Winter Solstice

Blessed is the road that keeps us homeless.
Blessed is the mountain that blocks our way.

Blessed are hunger and thirst, loneliness and all forms of desire.
Blessed is the labor that exhausts us without end.

Blessed are the night and the darkness that blinds us.
Blessed is the cold that teaches us to feel.

Blessed are the cat, the child, the cricket, and the crow.
Blessed is the hawk devouring the hare.

Blessed are the saint and the sinner who redeem each other.
Blessed are the dead, calm in their perfection.

Blessed is the pain that humbles us.
Blessed is the distance that bars our joy.

Blessed is this shortest day that makes us long for light.
Blessed is the love that in losing we discover.

Seven Deadly Sins

Forget about the other six, says Pride.
They're only using you.
Admittedly, Lust is a looker,
but you can do better.

And why do they keep bringing us
to this cheesy dive?
The food's so bad that even Gluttony
can't finish his meal.

Notice how Avarice
keeps refilling his glass
whenever he thinks we're not looking,
while Envy eyes your plate.

Hell, we're not even done, and Anger
is already arguing about the bill.
I'm the only one who
ever leaves a decent tip.

Let them all go, the losers!
It's a relief to see Sloth's
fat ass go out the door.
But stick around. I have a story

that not everyone appreciates—
about the special satisfaction
of staying on board as the last
grubby lifeboat pushes away.

Maryann Corbett (1950)

Maryann Corbett's poems honor the poetic tradition in English, with its multiplicity of received forms, while innovating within the flexible parameters of that tradition. Even within the set boundaries of the Petrarchan sonnet, with its fourteen lines and its repeated rhymes, she is continually "making it new." "State Fair Fireworks, Labor Day," for example, proceeds from epiphany to epiphany. The material, sensory details of a fireworks display— "blazing chrysanthemums" that "shriek into bloom above the Tilt-a-Whirls," the crushed sweating bodies that watch these flowers roar into flame on the dark air—point to larger revelations. "All revels end." In the limited, form-framed world of the poem, as in our own lived experience, everything about that world on the brink of its autumn is vivid, immediate, and concretely present, yet all that reality dissolves on the air like smoke. Without direct reference to Scripture, the poem declares: *The grass withers, the flower fades*—and leaves the rest to resonate unspoken.

In "Holiday Concert," the form is looser: unrhymed tercets in a pentameter, or five-stress line, with a single line at the end, whose "night . . . sleet ... hideous lunchroom chairs" recall the concrete details in the first two stanzas, the stage on which children make themselves ardently vulnerable. The repeated exhortation, "Forgive us," contributes to the circularity of the poem's trajectory. Though the poem might read as gently organized free verse, it bears the imprint of traditional repetitive tercet forms like the villanelle or Dante's terza rima. This latter seems relevant, given the hellish quality of the setting—the ugly fluorescent lighting, the other children snickering at the intense concentration of the little girl wielding cymbals—and the suggestion that those who forget the humiliations of the school concert are doomed to repeat them. Here the Christian vision illuminates a contemporary and immediate hell.

Born in 1950, Maryann Corbett spent many years as a master indexer for the Minnesota State Legislature before beginning her career as a poet in the early 2000s. She is, to date, the author of six collections of poetry. A prolific translator as well, she works with texts in Latin, Old English, French, and Old Occitan. She has received the Lyric Memorial Prize, the Willis Barnstone Translation Prize, and the Richard Wilbur Book Award, and has been a finalist for the Able Muse Book Award and the Howard Nemerov Sonnet Award.

STATE FAIR FIREWORKS, LABOR DAY

Look up: blazing chrysanthemums in rose
shriek into bloom above the Tilt-a-Whirls,
hang for a blink, then die in smoky swirls.

They scream revolt at what the body knows:
all revels end. We clap and sigh. Then, no—
another rose! another peony! break,
flame, roar, as though by roaring they might make
the rides whirl in perpetuum. As though
we need not finally, wearily turn, to plow
back through the crush of bodies, the lank air,
to buses that inch us, sweating, across town.
As though we were not dropped in silence there
to trudge the last blocks home, the streetlamps low,
the crickets counting summer's seconds down.

Holiday Concert

Forgive us. We have dragged them into the night
in taffeta dresses, in stiff collars and ties,
with the wind damp, the sleet raking their cheeks,

to school lunchrooms fitted with makeshift stages
where we will sit under bad fluorescent lighting
on folding chairs, and they will sing and play.

We will watch the first grader with little cymbals,
bending her knees, hunched in concentration
while neighbors snicker at her ardent face.

Forgive us. We will hear the seventh-grade boy
as his voice finally loses its innocence
forever, at the unbearable solo moment

and know that now, for years, he will wince at the thought
of singing, yet will ache to sing, in silence,
silence even to the generation to come

with its night, its sleet, its hideous lunchroom chairs.

Timothy Murphy (1951–2018)

Timothy Murphy was born in 1951 in Hibbing, Minnesota, but grew up in the Red River Valley of North Dakota. He graduated from Yale in 1972, where he studied under Robert Penn Warren and was a Scholar in the House of Poetry. He returned to North Dakota after graduation and became a partner in a seven-state hog farm that produced 850,000 hogs a year at its height. Raised Catholic, Murphy returned to the Church in 2005, a year after his plan to shoot himself was dramatically interrupted by a call from a friend who had become a priest.

Murphy's poetry, written in easy-flowing meter and loose end rhyme, is both autobiographical and devotional. He writes about his friends, hunting (a favorite topic), his dogs, priests, and Catholic feasts and saints. Like William Wordsworth, he believes that a poet is "a man speaking to men," not just to other poets. His poems are meant to be memorized and recalled as occasion permits, which gives them an odd singularity in a period marked by performative abstruseness. The Scottish editor and critic Gerry Cambridge wrote in a review of Murphy's first volume of poems, *The Deed of Gift*, that "It would be hard to confuse Murphy with any other contemporary poet. No one else writing poetry in English sounds quite like him." For Murphy, simplicity is a characteristic of intelligence and beauty. Thus, in a poem like "Hunter's Grace," he is unafraid to write: "For crops in our fields, / for the cocks in our crops, / good dogs, straight shooting, / we thank thee, great God."

At the same time, his work is also marked by an interest in paradox in the line of John Donne and Gerard Manley Hopkins, both examples. Included in this volume are "Open the Way," which begins: "Open the Way for God? Take to the road," and "Agapé," a poem about a dream Murphy had the night Pope John Paul II died. In the poem, Murphy writes about the Church that has both done him violence (Murphy was raped by a Jesuit priest as a teenager) and shown him the love of God. It closes with the Pope appearing to Murphy at hunting camp and declaring "*Te Dominus amat*"—"God loves you."

Murphy is the author of four volumes of poetry, a translation of Beowulf, which he completed with his longtime partner Alan Sullivan, and a memoir in verse and prose titled *Set the Ploughshare Deep*. He died from cancer in 2018.

AGAPÉ

The night you died, I dreamed you came to camp
to hear confession from an Eagle Scout
tortured by forty years of sin and doubt.
You whispered vespers by a hissing lamp.

Handlers, allowing you to hike with me,
followed us to the Bad Axe waterfront
down a firebreak this camper used to hunt.
Through all I said you suffered silently.

I blamed the authors of my unbelief:
St. Paul, who would have deemed my love obscene,
the Jesuit who raped me as a teen,
the altar boy when I was six, the grief

of a child chucked from Eden, left for dead
by Peter's Church and all the choirs above.
In a thick Polish accent choked with love,
Te Dominus amat[31] was all you said.

PRAYER FOR SOBRIETY

Morning glories climbing the garden wall
vie with the fragrant jasmine to outshine
the sun emerging from a summer squall.
Blossom and vine, lover and love entwine.
He is the Groom, and I? The shy betrothed
enraptured by the faith I so long loathed.

This is the sacramental cup we drink,
this the unleavened loaf on which we dine,
deliverance from the sins to which I sink.
Here is the book, the work of my Divine
Redeemer at whose Word the worlds revolve.
Let me return His passion with resolve.

---

31 Murphy's note on this poem reads as follows: "Pope John Paul II died on April 2, 2005, and
that night he visited me in a dream. This dream recurred three times. The last time was April 15,
2007—the night Pope Benedict XVI accosted American bishops over the matter of clerical sexual
abuse—when this poem came to me in its entirety. I rose and immediately typed it. In every
instance the dream was identical, and John Paul's words were the same. *Te Dominus amat* is Latin
for 'God loves you.'"

HUNTER'S GRACE

For the crops in our fields,
for the cocks in our crops,
good dogs, straight shooting,
we thank thee, great God.

SOUL OF THE NORTH

Out of the wilds, I pray.
Bound by my northern birth
to fish, to hunt the earth
and follow my forebears' way,
I mutter I have sinned,
wander the knee-high grass,
flourish awhile and pass
whistling into the wind.

As char swim to the clear
tundra rivers that run
under the midnight sun,
as wolves follow the deer
drawn from ford to ford,
as clamorous geese in V's
throng to the thawing seas—
all creatures of one accord—
my soul thirsts for the Lord.

PRAYER FOR PENTECOST

I pray for each good priest
who subjugates his will
to yours, who lays your feast
before me. Savior, still
the whirlwinds in their breasts.
Steady them for their tests.
Lord, hear my prayer.

I pray for virtuous men
who never knew your grace.
Each night I plead again,
"Let them behold your face,
love them with your elect."
I pray for Anthony Hecht.
Lord, hear my prayer.

My prayer list for the ill
changes as old friends die,
as my coevals fill
their swelling ranks, and I
whom you have spared so long,
old as I am, stay strong.
Lord, hear my prayer.

Lastly I pray for me,
a sinner so long lost,
so blind, I couldn't see
the tongues of Pentecost
descending all ablaze
to teach me thanks and praise.
Lord, hear my prayer.

OPEN THE WAY

Open the Way for God? Take to the road,
Calvary Hill. It is no easy path.
Give up your greed, your tendency to wrath,
go to confession, and lay down your load.

Turn your attention from your sad sack self
to those around you, suffering and in need.
Let no day pass without a kindred deed,
take down the King James Bible from your shelf,

drink deeply, grow like Jeremiah's tree
beside a stream; it flourishes in drought
and casts its shade on all beset by doubt
who follow the hard trail from misery,

hatred of self and others, mortal fright
and suicidal darkness into light.

Andrew Hudgins (1951)

Andrew Hudgins was born in Killeen, Texas, and was raised in a military family. As a child, he lived in many places across the United States before his family settled in Montgomery, Alabama, where Hudgins attended high school and college—graduating from both Huntingdon College and the University of Alabama. His home was a religious one—his father was as a deacon in the local Baptist church—and Hudgins made a profession of faith when his family was living in California (though he would change the location to Alabama in his poem "When I Was Saved"). Hudgins had a crisis of faith in college, and he has written about his discomfort with Christianity in his 2010 essay "Some Paradoxes of Religious Poetry." Hudgins writes: "Though I have been called a Christian poet and may even, once or twice, have called myself one, I'm not sure I'd invite myself to the party. . . . When I was child I prayed fervently for a call from God. I yearned then as I still do for the comfort of a faith. But I was also terrified I'd actually receive that call and have to give my whole being over to God."

The problem for Hudgins is a longstanding one for many Christians, especially those of a more pietistic bent. His awareness—and it is one that he expresses regularly in his poetry—that he is a divided self and possesses an imperfect or merely cursory satisfaction in the person of Christ erodes his confidence in his assent. This is what he seems to acknowledge when he writes that "There may be a middle path between endless, unvarying abnegation before God on one hand and blithe apostasy on the other, but the preachers I heard, with solid biblical authority, assured me there is not. They were wrong of course, but the doubt lingers."

Hudgins's poetry is, among other things, a poetry for doubters who nevertheless believe or want to believe. It reminds us that while we are capable of fleeting moments of self-possession, we are, at root, alienated from ourselves, others, creation, and—experientially if not ontologically—God. He puts the problem this way in "How Shall We Sing the Lord's Song in a Strange Land?": "This world, / this world is home. But it / will never feel like home." His poetry stands against triumphalism—Christian or secular—as we see in "Raven Days." What can we learn from the raven—that "ambiguous bird"? For Hudgins: He fed Elijah, "and doing so fed all of us," but he also "knows his way around a desert / and a corpse, and these are useful skills."

If Hudgins's poetry is for doubters, it is also for those with a healthy sense of humor. Life is tragic *and* comedic—things, for seemingly no reason whatsoever (call it grace), sometimes turn out okay. Christ rises from the grave and ascends in "Christ as Gardener": "Beneath his feet, seeds dance into the air." A second marriage is better than the first in "Babylon in a Jar," and a drunk prays for mercy in "Praying Drunk": "As I fall past, remember me." For Hudgins, humor is a form of truth telling. The author of a memoir on jokes and a collection of humorous children's poems, Hudgins told NPR that "there's a kind of disparity between what we're told and what we're witnessing, and jokes often love those kinds of contradictions." Hudgins's takes aim at this disparity in his sardonic "Beatitudes," which is included in this volume.

The author of nine collections of poetry and three works of nonfiction, Hudgins is emeritus Humanities Distinguished Professor of English at Ohio State University. He has been a finalist for both the Pulitzer Prize for Poetry and the National Book Award. The recipient of the Hanes Poetry Prize, Witter Bynner Award for Poetry, two grants from the National Endowment for the Arts, and a Guggenheim fellowship, he was inducted into the Fellowship of Southern Writers in 2007.

RAVEN DAYS

These are what my father calls
our raven days. The phrase is new
to me. I'm not sure what it means.
If it means we're hungry, it's right.
If it means we live on carrion,
it's right. It's also true
that every time we raise a voice
to sing, we make a caw and screech,
a raucous keening for the dead,
of whom we have more than our share.
But the raven's an ambiguous bird.
He forebodes death, and yet he fed
Elijah in the wilderness
and doing so fed all of us.
He knows his way around a desert
and a corpse, and these are useful skills.

HOW SHALL WE SING THE LORD'S SONG IN A STRANGE LAND?

We crept up, watched a black
man shovel dry burst of dirt
into the air. Engrossed,
he didn't see me till
my friend hawked hard and then
stepped out of sight. The man
jerked back, convinced I'd come
to spit on him. Held there
by guilt that wasn't fairly mine,
I braced for what he'd say.
Instead, he smiled, forgave
the sin I hadn't sinned
and turned back to his work.
I stumbled off and yelled,
goddamn you at my friend,
who laughed. Behind us, sand
exploded from the hole, caught wind,
and drifted slowly down
past headstones. Within a month
two boys found the black man hanging
from a hickory, his face
vague in a mist of gnats.
and every time they told the story
the gnats grew thicker, fiercer.
But I believed. I ached
the guiltless ache of dreams
and shuddered. A family that
I never saw mourned him.
Their lives changed and that change
spread out past my small-boy
imagining — though I
tried hard to follow it,
at twelve already remembering
how, ten years old, I'd stand
before the mirror and aim

a flashlight in my mouth.
White cheeks glowed red. I knew
that when I flicked the switch
I would no longer shine
with bloodlight, like stained glass.
I would return to the flesh
I'd always been. Back then,
I thought that if I could
I'd forgive nothing—I'd
change everything. But that's
before I learned how we
get trapped inside the haunts
and habits of this world.
While we drink coffee, gossip,
my cousin's daughter pounds on
the piano. It drives me nuts.
But Ellen's used to it.
The child plays till she drops,
and then we lug her
—elongated and limp—to bed.
My cousin tucks her in,
chooses one music box
from dozens on a shelf, winds it,
and sets it by her child's
damp head. The girl hums, drifts
from one world she creates
into another. A dark
circle of drool surrounds her head.
My cousin loves her with
the tenderness we save
for something that will ruin
our lives, break us, nail
us irretrievably
into this world, which we,
like good philosophers,
had meant to hate. This world,
this world is home. But it
will never feel like home.

Praying Drunk

Our Father who art in heaven, I am drunk.
Again. Red wine. For which I offer thanks.
I ought to start with praise, but praise
comes hard to me. I stutter. Did I tell you
about the woman whom I taught, in bed,
this prayer? It starts with praise; the simple form
keeps things in order. I hear from her sometimes.
Do you? And after love, when I was hungry,
I said, *Make me something to eat.* She yelled,
Poof! You're a casserole!—and laughed so hard
she fell out of the bed. Take care of her.

Next, confession—the dreary part. At night
deer drift from the dark woods and eat my garden.
They're like enormous rats on stilts except,
of course, they're beautiful. But why? What *makes*
them beautiful? I haven't shot one yet.
I might. When I was twelve, I'd ride my bike
out to the dump and shoot the rats. It's hard
to kill your rats, our Father. You have to use
a hollow point and hit them solidly.
A leg is not enough. The rat won't pause.
Yeep! Yeep! it screams, and scrabbles, three-legged, back
into the trash, and I would feel a little bad
to kill something that wants to live
more savagely than I do, even if
it's just a rat. My garden's vanishing.
Perhaps I'll merely plant more beans, though that
might mean more beautiful and hungry deer.
Who knows?
            I'm sorry for the times I've driven
home past a black, enormous, twilight ridge.
Crested with mist, it looked like a giant wave
about to break and sweep across the valley,
and in my loneliness and fear I've thought,
O let it come and wash the whole world clean.

Forgive me. This is my favorite sin: despair—
whose love I celebrate with wine and prayer.

Our Father, thank you for all the birds and trees,
that nature stuff. I'm grateful for good health,
food, air, some laughs, and all the other things
I'm grateful that I've never had to do
without. I have confused myself. I'm glad
there's not a rattrap large enough for deer.
While at the zoo last week, I sat and wept
when I saw one elephant insert his trunk
into another's ass, pull out a lump,
and whip it back and forth impatiently
to free the goodies hidden in the lump.
I could have let it mean most anything,
but I was stunned again at just how little
we ask for in our lives. *Don't look! Don't look!*
Two young nuns tried to herd their giggling
schoolkids away. *Line up,* they called. *Let's go
and watch the monkeys in the monkey house.*
I laughed, and got a dirty look. Dear Lord,
we lurch from metaphor to metaphor,
which is—let it be so—a form of praying.

I'm usually asleep by now—the time
for supplication. Requests. As if I'd stayed
up late and called the radio and asked
they play a sentimental song. Embarrassed.
I want a lot of money and a woman.
And, also, I want vanishing cream. You know—
a character like Popeye rubs it on
and disappears. Although you see right through him,
he's there. He chuckles, stumbles into things,
and smoke that's clearly visible escapes
from his invisible pipe. It makes me think,
sometimes, of you. What makes me think of me
is the poor jerk who wanders out on air
and then looks down. Below his feet, he sees
eternity, and suddenly his shoes

no longer work on nothingness, and down
he goes. As I fall past, remember me.

CHRIST AS A GARDENER

The boxwoods planted in the park spelled LIVE.
I never noticed it until they died.
Before, the entwined green had smudged the word
unreadable. And when they take their own advice
again—come spring, come Easter—no one will know
a word is buried in the leaves. I love the way
that Mary thought her resurrected Lord
a gardener. It wasn't just the broad-brimmed hat
and muddy robe that fooled her: He was that changed.
He looks across the unturned field, the riot
of unscythed grass, the smattering of wildflowers.
Before he can stop himself, he's on his knees.
He roots up stubborn weeds, pinches the suckers,
deciding order here—what lives, what dies,
and how. But it goes deeper even than that.
His hands burn and his bare feet smolder. He longs
to lie down inside the long, dew-moist furrows
and press his pierced side and his broken forehead
into the dirt. But he's already done it—
passed through one death and out the other side.
He laughs. He kicks his bright spade in the earth
and turns it over. Spring flashes by, then harvest.
Beneath his feet, seeds dance into the air.
They rise, and he, not noticing, ascends
on midair steppingstones of dandelion,
of milkweed, thistle, cattail, and goldenrod.

BEATITUDES

Blessed is the Eritrean child,
flies rooting at his eyes for moisture. Blessed
the remote control with which I flipped on past.
Blessed the flies whose thirst is satisfied.
Blessed the parents, too weak to brush away
the vibrant flies.
           Blessed the camera crew
and blessed the gravity of Dan Rather, whose voice
grows stranger with every death he sees. Blessed
my silence and my wife's as we chewed our hot
three-cheese lasagna.
           Blessed the comedies
we watched that night, the bed we slept in, the work
we rose to and completed before we sat
once more to supper before the television
a day during which the one child died
and many like him. Blessed is the small check
we wrote and mailed. Blessed is our horror.

Mark Jarman (1952)

Poetry, writes Mark Jarman in the preface to *Dailiness: Essays on Poetry,* "celebrates being alive as an act of consciousness." He continues: "When in the Book of Genesis, God says, 'Let there be light,' it is like saying let me see what I am making, let me give myself a place where there is time, and I think about what I am doing . . . God is the first poet or maker." *Acts of consciousness,* in *a place where there is time,* in which the maker *thinks about what he is doing:* this intensity of generative attention characterizes Jarman's poetry. His poems constitute imaginative enterings into a recognizable reality bounded by time and space, with solid ground on which a reader might set his or her feet.

The boundaries of time and space, and the pressure that those boundaries exert on experience, are hallmarks of narrative, a defining quality in Jarman's poetry. As co-editor, with Robert McDowell, of the literary journal *The Reaper,* in the nineteen-eighties, Jarman became an influential voice in the New Narrative Movement, arguing for a poetry rooted in realism, in the concrete imagery of lived human experience, rather than in "the weather in my head," as McDowell once strikingly put it. For Jarman, this emphasis on the narrative came to dovetail as well with the New Formalist Movement's impulse toward rhyme, meter, and other traditional boundary markers for poetry.

Jarman's sense of poetic integrity—that there are identifiable, non-arbitrary things a poem should do and be, if it is to call itself a poem—mirrors his own poems' insistence on larger integrities of meaning and truth. Throughout his career, his poems have interrogated his own experience, with particular emphasis on his life as the son of a clergyman, offered a set of religious principles that cannot become his own without intense examination. His poems set themselves the task of discerning what is true, in order to articulate both the truth and the experience of discerning it. If God says, *Let me think about what I am doing,* then Jarman's poems bear that image, the maker thinking about what he does as he does it.

The first of Jarman's *Unholy Sonnets*—whose collective title alludes to the *Holy Sonnets* of the metaphysical poet John Donne—sets out precisely this proposition: to think about God, though thinking about God is intrinsically problematic. "I can say almost anything about you, / O Big Idea, and with each epithet, / Create new reasons to believe or doubt you." The sonnet feels its way forward, testing "each epithet" for God, as one might test the thickness of the ice on the pond, and finding it not entirely adequate. "You / Solve nothing but the problems that I set," the poem concludes. In more narrative poems, meanwhile, such as "Questions for Ecclesiastes," Jarman posits impossible situations, as when a minister must find something to say to parents whose teenaged daughter has shot herself, a problem though which the poem must think itself toward some resolution, however complicated, open-ended, and ultimately unreached—as from the timebound human world, God himself is ultimately unreachable. It is too often a glib truism that God's seeming refusal to answer prayers constitutes an answer; Jarman's poems assert, rather, in the words of his "Unholy Sonnet 4," that

This God recedes from every metaphor,
Turns the hardest data into untruth,
And fills all blanks with blankness. This love shows
Itself in absence, which the stars adore.

Born in Sterling, Kentucky, in 1952, Mark Jarman spent his childhood between Southern California and Scotland, where his father, a minister of the Disciples of Christ, was called as part of a mission to British churches. Educated at the University of California, Santa Cruz, and the Iowa Writers' Workshop, he has taught at Indiana State University, Evansville; the University of California, Irvine; Murray State University; and from 1983 to 2020, Vanderbilt University, where he holds the title of Centennial Professor of English Emeritus. His honors include the Balcones Poetry Prize, the Lenore Marshall Poetry Prize of the Academy of American Poets, a Guggenheim Fellowship, and multiple grants and fellowships from the National Endowment for the Arts. He is the author of eleven books of poetry, most recently *The Heronry,* published in 2017. In addition to *The Reaper Essays,* with Robert McDowell, Jarman has also published three collections of essays on poetry: *The Secret of Poetry, Body and Soul,* and *Dailiness.*

QUESTIONS FOR ECCLESIASTES

What if on a foggy night in a beachtown, a night when
    the Pacific leans close like the face of a wet cliff, a
    preacher were called to the house of a suicide, a
    house of strangers, where a child had discharged a
    rifle through the roof of her mouth and the top of
    her skull?

What if he went to the house where the parents, stunned
    into plaster statues, sat behind their coffee table,
    and what if he assured them that the sun would rise
    and go down, the wind blow south, then turn north,
    whirling constantly, rivers—even the concrete flume
    of the great Los Angeles—run into the sea, and four-
    teen year old girls would manage to spirit themselves
    out of life, nothing was new under the sun?

What if he said the eye is not satisfied with seeing, nor the
    ear filled with hearing? Would he want to view the
    bedroom vandalized by self-murder or hear the
    quiet before the tremendous shout of the gun or the

people inside the shout, shouting or screaming,
crying and pounding to get into the room, kicking
through the hollow-core door and making a new
sound and becoming a new silence—the silence he
entered with his comfort?

What if as comfort he said to the survivors I praise the
dead which are dead already more than the living,
and better is he than both dead and living who is
not yet alive? What if he folded his hands together
and ate his own flesh in prayer? For he did pray
with them. He asked them, the mother and the father, if
they wished to pray to do so in any way they felt
comfortable, and the father knelt at the coffee table
and the mother turned to squeeze her eyes into a
corner of the couch, and they prayed by first listen-
ing to his prayer, then clawing at his measured
cadences with tears (the man cried) and curses (the
woman swore). What if, then, the preacher said be
not rash with thy mouth and let not thine heart be
hasty to utter anything before God: for God is in
heaven?

What if the parents collected themselves, then, and asked
him to follow them to their daughter's room, and
stood at the shattered door, the darkness of the
room beyond, and the father reached in to put his
hand on the light switch and asked if the comforter,
the preacher they were meeting for the first time in
their lives, would like to see the aftermath, and
instead of recoiling and apologizing, he said that
the dead know not anything for the memory of
them is forgotten? And while standing in the hall-
way, he noticed the shag carpet underfoot, like the
fur of a cartoon animal, the sort that requires comb-
ing with a plastic rake, leading into the bedroom,
where it would have to be taken up, skinned off the
concrete slab of the floor, and still he said for their
love and hatred and envy are now perished, neither

have the dead any more portion for ever in anything
that is done under the sun?

What if as an act of mercy so acute it pierced the preacher's
skull and traveled the length of his spine, the man
did not make him regard the memory of his daugh-
ter as it must have filled her room, but guided the
wise man, the comforter, to the front door, with his
wife with her arms crossed before her in that ges-
ture we use to show a stranger to the door, acting
out a rite of closure, compelled to be social, as we
try to extricate ourselves by breaking off the exten-
sions of our bodies, as raccoons gnaw their legs from
traps, turning aside our gaze, letting only the numb
tissue of valedictory speech ease us apart, and the
preacher said live joyfully all the days of the life of
thy vanity, for that is thy portion in this life?

They all seem worse than heartless, don't they, these stark
and irrelevant platitudes, albeit stoical and final,
oracular, stony, and comfortless? But they were at
the center of that night, even if they were unspoken.

And what if one with only a casual connection to the
tragedy remembers a man, younger than I am today,
going out after dinner and returning, then sitting in
the living room, drinking a cup of tea, slowly
finding the strength to say he had visited these
grieving strangers and spent some time with them?

Still that night exists for people I do not know in ways I do
not know, though I have tried to imagine them. I
remember my father going out and my father com-
ing back. The fog, like the underskin of a broken
wave, made a low ceiling that the street lights
pierced and illuminated. And God who shall bring
every work into judgment, with every secret thing,
whether it be good or whether it be evil, who could
have shared what he knew with people who needed
urgently to hear it, God kept a secret.

UNHOLY SONNET I

Dear God, our Heavenly Father, Gracious Lord,
Mother Love and Maker, Light Divine,
Atomic Fingertip, Cosmic Design,
First Letter of the Alphabet, Last Word,
Mutual Satisfaction, Cash Award,
Auditor Who Approves Our Bottom Line,
Examiner Who Says That We Are Fine,
Oasis That All Sands Are Running Toward.

I can say almost anything about you,
O Big Idea, and with each epithet,
Create new reasons to believe or doubt you,
Black Hole, White Hole, Presidential Jet.
But what's the anything I must leave out? You
Solve nothing but the problems that I set.

UNHOLY SONNET II

Half asleep in prayer I said the right thing
And felt a sudden pleasure come into
The room or my own body. In the dark,
Charged with a change of atmosphere, at first
I couldn't tell my body from the room.
And I was wide awake, full of this feeling,
Alert as though I'd heard a doorknob twist,
A drawer pulled, and instead of terror knew
The intrusion of an overwhelming joy.
I had said thanks and this was the response.
But how I said it or what I said it for
I still cannot recall and I have tried
All sorts of ways all hours of the night.
Once was enough to be dissatisfied.

REMINDER

For God is in heaven, and you upon earth.
    —Ecclesiastes 5:2

Don't take your eyes off the road.
Accept nothing as given.
Watch where you put your hands.
You're here and God's in heaven.

Be careful where you step.
The drop-off's somewhere near.
The fog won't lift tonight.
God's in heaven. You're here.

That word you wish to say,
That score you'd like to even—
Don't hurry either while
You're here and God's in heaven.

The earth says, "Take the wheel.
But no matter how you steer,
I'll still go round in circles.
God's in heaven. You're here."

HYMN

"Great is thy faithfulness,"
    Say the leaves to the light.
"Oh God, my father,"
    Says darkness to night.

"There is no shadow,"
    Says the eye to the sun.
"Of turning with thee,"
    As tears start to burn.

"All I have needed,"
    Says the sand to the storm.
"Thy hand has provided,"
    Say the combs to the swarm.

"Great is thy faithfulness,"
    Says the cup to the brim.
"Lord unto me,"
    Say I unto him.

Franz Wright (1953–2015)

Franz Wright converted to Catholicism in 1999. This marked a subtle but significant shift in his work. Wright's poetry has always addressed life's suffering and loneliness head on. Following Rilke, he conceives of the poet as an empty "bottle" that "sings / when you blow into its lips." It is the poet's emptiness—his suffering—that makes the beautiful note possible. His early work is haunted by "voices" and is often addressed to a "you," who is sometimes his late father, the poet James Wright. In his early work, images of snow and moments of silence—captured on the page in large spaces between stanzas—are metaphors for the meaninglessness of life. The act of writing is a temporary means of vanquishing the whiteness of silence and establishing a fleeting communion with others.

A shift begins to take shape in *Rorschach Test* (1995), where the poet admits "I have been attempting to pray / the Lord's Prayer for the first time / since I was a child." This first attempt ends in failure. "Hope," Wright writes in another poem in the volume, is "that obscene cruelty, it never lets up for a / minute." He determines to leave hope alone: "If the telephone / rings just don't answer it," and he writes in "Church of the Strangers" that "There are no symbols / with the efficacy we require." Yet, within a few years, he changed his view. *Walking to Martha's Vineyard* (2005) begins with the announcement of faith in "Year One," and he writes in "Baptism" that "*Your* words are spirit / and life. / Only say one / and he will be healed."

The silence of his early work is transformed in the later volumes. No longer is it a symbol for the underlying emptiness of life but of the inscrutable but omnipresent being of God, who speaks and acts in Christ and whose suffering, unlike the suffering of the poet, offers healing and meaning. The recurring phrase, "I have heard the silence of God," in *God's Silence* (2006) points to the paradox of an inscrutable but self-revealing God who is the Word but who cannot be captured in language. Wright's work is still unflinchingly honest about life's suffering and his own failures, but we also find ecstasy in God's forgiveness and love. "There is hope in the past," Wright writes in "P. S.", and in "I, for One," he states: "I am so glad // there is no fear, / and finally I can // ask no second life."

Wright earned a BA from Oberlin College and was the recipient of a Guggenheim Fellowship and a grant from the National Endowment for the Arts. He is the author of twelve volumes of poetry, including *Walking to Martha's Vineyard*, which won the 2004 Pulitzer Prize for poetry. He died in 2015 at the age of 62.

Year One

I was still standing
on a northern corner.

Moonlit winter clouds the color of the desperation of wolves.

Proof
of Your existence? There is nothing
but.

One Heart

It is late afternoon and I have just returned from
the longer version of my walk nobody knows
about. For the first time in nearly a month, and
everything changed. It is the end of March, once
more I have lived. This morning a young woman
described what it's like shooting coke with a baby
in your arms. The astonishing windy and altering light
and clouds and water were, at certain moment,
You.

There is only one heart in my body, have mercy
on me.

The brown leaves buried all winter creatureless feet
running over dead grass beginning to green, the first scent-
less violet here and there, returned, the first star noticed all
at once as one stands staring into the black water.

Thank You for letting me live for a little as one of the
sane; thank You for letting me know what this is
like. Thank You for letting me look at your frightening
blue sky without fear, and your terrible world without
terror, and your loveless psychotic and hopelessly
lost
    with this love.

BAPTISM

That insane asshole is dead
I drowned him
and he's not coming back. Look
he has a new life
a new name
now
which no one knows except
the one who gave it.

If he tastes
the wine now
as he is allowed to
it won't, I'm not saying it
will
turn to water

however, since You
can do anything, he
will be safe

his first breath as an infant
past the waters of birth
and his soul's, past the death water, married—

Your words are spirit
and life.
Only say one
and he will be healed.

THE HAWK

Maybe in a million years
a better form of human
being will come, happier
and more intelligent. A few already
have infiltrated this world and lived
to very much regret it,

I suppose.
          Me,
I'd prefer to have come
in the form of that hawk, floating over
the mirroring fire
of Clearlake's
hill, my gold
skull filled with nothing
but God's will
the whole day through, instead
of these glinting voices incessantly
unerringly guiding me
to pursue
what makes me sick, and not to
what makes me glad. And yet
I am changing: this three-pound lump
of sentient meat electrified
by hope and terror has learned to hear
His silence like the sun,
and sought to change!
And friends
on earth at the same time
as me, listen: from the sound of those crickets
last night, René Char said
prenatal life
must have been sweet—
each voice perhaps also a star
in that night
from which
this time
we won't be
interrupted anymore—but
fellow monsters while we are still here, for one minute, think
about this: there is someone right now who is looking
to you, not Him, for whatever
love still exists.

After Absence

God's words translated into human words
are spoken and shine
on a few upturned faces.

There is nothing else like this.

I will tell you what no eye has seen
and teach you to see
what no ear has heard—

Father

and,
vine
of my blood.

Forgive me
the harm I have done

Those who have harmed me
forgive . . .

They say what we are going to be
will not become clear
until he appears

and when this happens
we will become like him
for we will see him as he is.

They say become passers-through.

God is love
they say,
in human words.

Marly Youmans (1953)

Like the contemporary Cornish poet Charles Causley (1917–2003), one of her influences, Marly Youmans touches even the most familiar narrative into mythic strangeness. In her hands the Gospel story of the Transfiguration, for example, evokes the moon as a coin—like the coin rendered unto Caesar—on which the head not of Caesar but of Christ, the "man awake beneath the sky," is struck in profile. Christ's dazzling raiment outshines this moon; "[h]is shape of light is wholly beautiful," the poem asserts, "and useless with the uselessness of art." In this poem, the mystery of the Transfiguration becomes both itself and more than itself, speaking not only to the revealed glory beheld by the apostles, but to created things whose very createdness is meant for nothing else than to reflect that glory, even as the moon reflects the sun. Art is

> … meant for nothing but the beautiful,
> That does nothing but transform utterly,
> And has no message to deliver
> But is the revelation of itself.

The Transfiguration, as the poem renders it, is an epiphany in which it becomes clear that Christ has come into the world not to *do*—not to overthrow Caesar, not to spearhead a revolution, not even to heal "the demon-raptured boy" whose distant howls end the poem—but to *be*, the *I AM*. It is his inexplicable glory which alone can transfigure and heal the world. If, as the poem suggests, art is sacramental and salvific, bearing into the world the image of that *I AM*, then its purpose, like Christ's, is ultimately simply to *be*.

Youmans's 2019 *The Book of the Red King*, meanwhile, not only re-narrates a mythos, but imagines one. In a folkloric city, the Red King rules from his tower, as peacemaker, book-writer, dreamer, creator. The Red King's Fool, a seeking figure, wandering in his own wilderness, registers a whole range of experience: humiliation, exaltation, longing, loss, all the registers of emotional and cognitive engagement that humanity entails. In "The Starry Fool," this pilgrim, entering the city, finds both his home and his mirroring, fully realized self, in the Red King's joyful welcome.

Born in 1953, the author of five volumes of poetry, Youmans has also published ten novels. Her honors include The Michael Shaara Award for Excellence in Civil War Fiction, the Theodore Hoepfner Award for the Short Story, the Ferrol Sams Award for Fiction, and a Yaddo Fellowship.

Transfiguration

Here are three sleepers on a mountaintop,
And here's a man awake beneath the sky—

Coinlike, the moonshine rims the profiled head.
And yet not moon but glimmerings of fire
That strengthen, shine like candlelight through snow
Until the face, the hands, and raiment seethe:
His shape of light is wholly beautiful
And useless with the uselessness of art
That's meant for nothing but the beautiful,
That does nothing but transform utterly
And has no message to deliver us
But is the revelation of itself.

Down in the gulf, a demon-raptured boy
Makes manifest the fallen world with howls.

THE STARRY FOOL

In a shivering of bells,
The Fool comes shining, shimmering
Unseen along the moonshine way.

Little fir trees sprinkle his path
With needles, lift their limbs and point
To the bright whirligigs of stars.

And the crack in the Fool's heart is
For once mended, without a seam:
He shakes his bell-branched staff at light.

So cold, no one plays the watchman,
But in the tower called *The Spear,*
The Red King rules the chiming hour.

He'll spy the moon-washed Fool, skittling
Like a toy top through the city.
He will run outside to greet him,

Calling, "My brother and my self,
My mirror, the crack inside my heart!"

Scott Cairns (1954)

Poetry is a participatory art for Scott Cairns. The poet's careful observation and precise description of the observable world do not illuminate truth as much as they partake of the eternal Word who made and sustains all things. As Cairns remarks in an interview with Mary Kenagy Mitchell for *Image*, poetry is an apprehension of "the vertiginous expanse of God's creation . . . a textured and inexhaustible reality that isn't circumscribed by expectations and intentions." In his introduction to Cairns's volume of collected poems, *Slow Pilgrim*, Gregory Wolfe writes that "Cairns has been on a lifelong pilgrimage in search of a way to live—and to create, as an artificer of words—that unites mind and heart, that achieves a true human wholeness."

The result of this view of poetry is a body of work marked by disarming humility, goofy sensuality, and open-handed joy. For Cairns, the poet is not a prophet as much as he is a pilgrim who uses words to reorient his life towards God in all God's mysteriousness. We see this in particular in Cairns's collection *Idiot Psalms*, comprised primarily of poems in the voice of a "slow" pilgrim, Isaak, which Cairns took as his saint name after Isaak of Syria, upon converting to Eastern Orthodoxy. In these poems, Isaak is a kind of holy fool, who confesses what we are often reticent to confess and asks God for things we are too embarrassed to ask:

> My enemies are plentiful, and I
>> surround them, these enemies
>> camped firmly in my heart, what passes,
>> lo these dreary ages, for my heart.

In other poems, Cairns turns to erotic love, where two united in one act and word is a symbol of Christ's incarnation and union with his Church. "I would like for us to find / again the faculty to apprehend / this eros honestly," Cairns writes in "Erotikos Logos," "and so to find / a way to meet in eros a likely / figure for most of what we do worth doing."

Cairns's view that poetry, like theology, is always apophatic—that is, concerned with what cannot be said—gives his work a power that is refreshingly free of tubthumping. In "Against Justice," for example, a poem that gets its title from a line in Saint Isaak of Syria, Cairns pushes back against facile descriptions of God's actions in terms of cause-and-effect, however comforting those descriptions might be. Rather than offering "what might pass for revelation," as some Christians do, Cairns instead concludes with tension: "The God / is hardly just," he writes, "and we are grateful for His oversight."

Cairns was born in Tacoma, Washington, and currently lives in University Place, Washington, where he directs Seattle Pacific University's low-residency MFA program in creative writing. Raised a Baptist, Cairns became a Presbyterian before converting to Eastern Orthodoxy in 1998. He has an MA from Hollins College, an MFA from Bowling Green State University, and a PhD from the University of Utah. Cairns won the Denise

Levertov Award in 2014 and has received fellowships from the National Endowment for the Humanities and the Guggenheim Foundation. His collections of poetry include *The Theology of Doubt*, *Philokalia*, *Idiot Psalms*, and *Slow Pilgrim: The Collected Poems*, among others. He is the author of the memoir *Short Trip to the Edge*, which tells the story of his trip to the monasteries of Mount Athos.

THE MORE EARNEST PRAYER OF CHRIST

And being in an agony he prayed more earnestly . . .
  —Luke 22:44

His last prayer in the garden began, as most
of his prayers began—*in earnest*, certainly,
but not without distraction, an habitual . . . what?

Distance? Well, yes, a sort of distance, or a mute
remove from the genuine distress he witnessed
in the endlessly grasping hands of multitudes

and, often enough, in his own embarrassing
circle of intimates. Even now, he could see
these where they slept, sprawled upon their robes or wrapped

among the arching olive trees. Still, something new,
unlikely, uncanny was commencing as he spoke.
As the divine in him contracted to an ache,

a throbbing in the throat, his vision blurred, his voice
grew thick and unfamiliar; his prayer—just before
it fell to silence—became uniquely earnest.

And in that moment—perhaps because it was so
new—he saw something, had his first taste of what
he would become, first pure taste of the body, and the blood.

POSSIBLE ANSWERS TO PRAYER

Your petitions—though they continue to bear
just the one signature—have been duly recorded.
Your anxieties—despite their constant,

relatively narrow scope and inadvertent
entertainment value—nonetheless serve
to bring your person vividly to mind.

Your repentance—all but obscured beneath
a burgeoning, yellow fog of frankly more
conspicuous resentment—is sufficient.

Your intermittent concern for the sick,
the suffering, the needy poor is sometimes
recognizable to me, if not to them.

Your angers, your zeal, your lipsmackingly
righteous indignation toward the many
whose habits and sympathies offend you—

these must burn away before you'll apprehend
how near I am, with what fervor I adore
precisely these, the several who rouse your passions.

BAD THEOLOGY: A QUIZ

And lo, the angel of the Lord came upon them,
and the glory of the Lord shone round about them:
and they were sore afraid.

Whenever we aver "the God is nigh,"
do we imply that He is ever otherwise?

When, in scripture, God's "anger" is said
to be aroused, just how do you take that?

If—whether now or in the fullness—we
stipulate that God is all in all, just where

or how would you position Hell? Which
is better—to break the law and soothe

the wounded neighbor, or to keep the law
and cause the neighbor pain? Do you mean it?

If another sins, what is that to you?
When the sinful suffer publicly, do you

find secret comfort in their grief, or will
you also weep? They are surely grieving;

are you weeping now? Assuming *sin* is *sin*,
whose do you condemn? Who is judge? Who

will feed the lambs? The sheep? Who, the goats?
Who will sell and give? Who will be denied?

Whose image haunts the mirror? And why
are you still here? What exactly do you hope

to become? When will you begin?

Idiot Psalm 2

A psalm of Isaak, accompanied by baying hounds.

O Shaper of varicolored clay and cellulose, O Keeper
        of same, O Subtle Tweaker, Agent
        of energies both appalling and unobserved,
        do not allow Your servant's limbs to stiffen
        or to ossify unduly, do not compel Your servant
        to go brittle, neither cramping at the heart,
        nor narrowing his affective sympathies
        neither of the flesh nor of the alleged soul.
Keep me sufficiently limber that I might continue
        to enjoy my morning run among the lilies
        and the rowdy waterfowl, that I might
        delight in this and every evening's intercourse
        with the woman you have set beside me.

Make me to awaken daily with a willingness
        to roll out readily, accompanied
        by grateful smirk, a giddy joy,
        the idiot's undying expectation,
        despite the evidence.

IDIOT PSALM 4

If I had anything approaching
        a new song, surely I would sing.

If I had sufficient vision,
        I would see.

If, amid the dim and dissolution
        of the January day, new music
        might avail to warm what passes
        for my heart, surely I would weep.

My enemies are plentiful, and I
        surround them, these enemies
        camped firmly in my heart, what passes,
        lo these dreary ages, for my heart.

O Lord of Hosts, do slay them.

DAWN AT SAINT ANNA'S SKETE
Agion Oros, 2006

The air is cool and is right thick with birdsong
as our bleary crew files out, of a sudden
disinterred from three sepulchral hours of prayer
into an amber brilliance rioting
outside the cemetery chapel. With bits
of Greek and English intermixed, the monks
invite us to the portico for coffee,
παξιμάδια,[32] a shot of cold ρακί.[33]
As I say, the air is cool, animate
and lit, and in such light the road already
beckons, so I skip the coffee, pound the shot,
and pocket two hard biscuits. And yes, the way
is broad at first, but narrows soon enough.

---

32 παξιμάδια — pahximáthia — Greek biscotti
33 ρακί — rahkeé — Greek grappa

Clare Rossini (1954)

Born in 1954 in St. Paul, Minnesota, Clare Rossini is the author of three books of poetry and co-editor of the recent anthology *The Poetry of Capital: Voices From Twenty-First Century America*. She has served as Artist-in-Residence at Trinity College in Hartford, Connecticut, where she also directs an arts-outreach program in the public schools, and as a faculty member for the Master of Fine Arts program in creative writing at the University of Vermont.

Rossini's loose-limbed free-verse poems are by turns wry and penetrating in their observations, conclusions, and questions. Her speaker in "Fra Angelico's 'Annunciation' at San Marco," a citizen of the material world, imagines Saint Dominic's reaching out to "finger" the angel's wing, to "let us know / what an angel's made of." But it is the mystical "cloud of unknowing"—from the medieval text describing a method of contemplative prayer in which the believer apprehends God, paradoxically, by letting go of everything he or she knows about God—that forms the substance of Rossini's poem "A Prayer of Sorts." The speaker here addresses God with colloquial familiarity, as one on sufficiently intimate terms with the Almighty to think aloud and struggle for the elusive right words: "Don't get me wrong . . . How to say it? . . . Let me put it this way." The thrust, in fact, is that words and images fall short, except to evoke negatives. "The nothingness you emanate," the poem begins, "the grand reserve / You're shawled up in, leaves us both / In the nether." The theme of the insufficiency of language might form its own sub-tradition within the larger tradition of religiously meditative poetry, but that insufficiency does not stop the speaker's asking the question at the heart of all religious questioning. "Day and night I finger your signs. / Were they faked? // Are *you*?" Here Rossini's speaker conflates two questions. Does God exist? And is God who he says he is, the *I AM*? The question "Are *you*?" turns that declaration on its head without ever asserting that "you" are *not*. The poem ends on a note of witty exasperation with God—"Don't make me / speak to clouds"—which both recalls the medieval "cloud of unknowing" and affirms, in the very act of speaking, that there is someone there to speak to.

Fra Angelico's "Annunciation" at San Marco

Imagine: an angel whose wings imply
The colors of the world. No wonder
Mary's head inclines, not wanting
To miss a word, her book half-dropped
From her hand in her surprise
At such a visitor.

If angels had not traditionally been
Thought of as male, one might mistake
These two for sisters: their plaster robes
Stained from the same palette of pink,
Their hair swept off their faces, falling
In similar curls.

But they keep their distance, as does Dominic,
The saint behind the pillar in the yard,
Who from the Renaissance looks on shyly,
His hands held formally in prayer,
His black and white habit austere
Next to the angel's wings, the venial
Pink lingering, not yet redeemed,
In Mary's cheek.

The monk whose cell this painting lit
Would take Brother Dominic's posture
As a model for his own when contemplating
This event, which looms with penitents
And spires. And probably, a prayerful stance
Is appropriate; how often, after all,
Are we promised saviors?

Still, it may have been more instructive
If the saint had been braver,
And reached out to finger those wings—
Just inches away—and let us know what
An angel's made of.

PRAYER OF SORTS

The nothingness you emanate,
The grand reserve
You're shawled up in, leaves us both
In the nether,

For which, don't get me wrong,
I've longed at times,
Fantasizing me
Bride of the Ineffable,
Call him night, mist, the genial
Zero himself.

Yet somehow it comes to this, our—
How to say it?—

"Relation"—

What do you seem? A shade
Vanished up the path, the path itself
Rolling up,
And the woods eating all.

I stew over your correspondences
Day and night, I finger your signs.
Were they faked?

Are *you?*

As it is, we walk on wires
Strung above vacuums. As it is, all words
Are yoked to the mute.

Let me put it this way:
The window frames a cumulus drifting.

Don't make me
Speak to clouds.

A. M. Juster (1956)

Poet and translator A. M. Juster is the author of ten books of poetry, translations, and satire, including *St. Aldhelm's Riddles,* a translation from the Latin of the Anglo-Saxon-era English bishop, and a book-length parody in the voice of the contemporary American poet Billy Collins. If in fact, as Hilaire Belloc has famously suggested, "Wherever the Catholic sun doth shine / There's always laughter and good red wine," Juster is the poet supplying the laughter. At the same time, his poems engage seriously, though often indirectly, with the Christian's large questions about the universe he inhabits and the God who runs it. Juster's poetic world, full of storms and ills, humiliations and betrayals, perils and waste, acknowledges, always, its own fallenness. Still, touched unexpectedly by grace, it sharpens into beauty.

"Japanese Maple," for example, celebrates grace as the triumph of the improbable. The delicate ornamental tree which a wife has insisted on planting, in the face of her husband's pragmatic, prosaic counsel, "flares with plum and amber lace" when other supposedly hardier trees are stripped bare. When ice destroys those others, "her gift keeps shimmering with fragile grace." Here the wise are made foolish, and foolish hope, which surely characterizes all gardening endeavors, is vindicated. In meek fragility, the maple inherits its measure of earth.

"Three Visitors," too, manifests the mysterious action of grace. The poem's tetrameter lines, borrowed from Old English verse, describe an ordinary winter night whose peace seems primed for a Grendel to plunder it. Here, the would-be Grendels are three coyotes on the prowl. Their number suggests those other strange "visitors," the Magi, though these travelers have not meant to visit the sleeping family. The poem's speaker knows better than to make more of this glimpse than it really means. "No star distracts their stealthy march," he remarks, as if to qualify the title's suggestion of the Magi as a fanciful overreach. No evident design has brought them there. They trot away, howling, toward the highway, where their own destruction might await them. Still, their path is rich with smells, the promise of good hunting. In this moment, they are utterly alive, living "things" whose truthful reclamation the poet has willed, making no more of them than they are, and no less. The world, if "awash" with wrath, remains still also "awash in wonder." Wrath may be the last word, but is never the only word.

Juster served for many years in the federal government, working for two White House administrations and serving as General Council at the U.S. Department of Health and Human Services. Currently, he is the poetry editor at *Plough Quarterly*. He is the winner of both the Howard Nemerov Sonnet Award and the Willis Barnstone Translation Prize.

JAPANESE MAPLE IN JANUARY

All spring she brushed aside my arguments
it would be cheaper, and would make more sense,
to fill the yard with hardy native stock.
She bought her maple, junked the chain-link fence,
and tried to start a lawn; our crabby flock
of grackles grew too fat on seed to quarrel.
While masons tamed the mud with slate and rock,
she planted birches, hollies and a laurel.
New pickets kept our neighbors in their place.

October stripped her birches down to bone,
as if to warn the weak. Beside new stone
the pygmy flares with plum and amber lace.
As ice storms make old oaks bow, crack and groan,
her gift keeps shimmering with fragile grace.

THREE VISITORS

Mist on moonspill   as midnight nears.
Adrift but not dreaming   our drowsy son
is covered and kissed.   At the kitchen door
our old basset is barking;   coyotes out back
are standing like statues   down by the dogwoods.
Across the crystal   of crusted snow,
they search for stragglers   to startle and chase.
Their vigil reveals   no victims this night.

Trash would be trouble;   they trot away
unbothered by bloodthroated   growling and baying.
No star distracts   their stealthy march.
As the highway hums   they howl through the calm,
then savor new scents   that spice their path
in this world awash   in wonder and wrath.

Bruce Beasley (1958)

Bruce Beasley was born in 1958 and spent his childhood in Macon, Georgia. He holds degrees from Oberlin College, Columbia University, and the University of Virginia. He teaches at Western Washington University in Bellingham, Washington, where in 2013 he was awarded the Peter J. Elich Excellence in Teaching Award. The author of eight books of poetry, he has received multiple Pushcart Prizes, a National Endowment for the Arts Fellowship, the 1994 Ohio State University Press / Journal Award for his second book, *The Creation*, the Colorado Prize for Poetry for his 1996 collection *Summer Mystagogia*, and the University of Georgia Contemporary Poetry Series Award for *Lord Brain* in 2005.

An obsessive curiosity animates Beasley's poems: not *obsessive* in the sense of *compulsive disorder*, but in the sense of the all-consuming desire for more knowledge that drives a child to stare at the caption to a picture of a dinosaur or a spacecraft until he finds he can make sense of the words. "I think of myself as a poet-cosmologist," Beasley has said, an apt self-description for the author of poems which both observe and probe the created universe and the possible mind behind it, in a relentless quest to find out how it all works. His poems are the natural outgrowth of a mind given to research and rumination, often enough on the oddities and paradoxes bound up in words themselves. As he remarked in a 2015 interview,

> Lately I've been obsessing over the German word *zerissenheit*, which means a state of dissolution or disunity, of being torn or self-divided, and which William James wonderfully translated as "Torn-to-pieces-hood." I've been thinking a lot about how words, when torn-to-pieces, reveal other words locked inside them.

I've been thinking a lot about is more or less what Beasley's poems say. That is, in their thinking, these poems find a friend in Thomas Aquinas, who would understand the drive to integrate disparate ideas and epiphanies into some whole, something not left torn-to-pieces, but touched again into unity.

"Consolation" exemplifies this urge toward unity even if, in the end, the soul whose strivings the poem chronicles remains "hankering and unhealed." In February—surely the true "cruelest month," whatever T. S. Eliot might say—the speaker finds his own spiritual brokenness echoed in the frozen "contract[ing]" and "crack[ing]" of the world. The soul itself has developed a crack, so that it cannot even perceive its own mirroring in the created order around it; in this contemporary rendering of the "Dialogue Between Self and Soul," the speaker has to tell his soul that this is the case.

> Here in the split kingdom
> of matter and spirit, the soul
> doesn't recognize itself

in its natural emblems

so I fill it in.

The *torn-to-pieces-hood* of the soul's perception of reality: therein lies the real spiritual problem. The speaker's Lenten project, then, is to restore some sense of wholeness. This he attempts through engagements not only with observations of winter phenomena, as they reflect his own interior state, but with such sources outside himself as William Paley's *Natural Theology,* the *Book of Job,* and the works of Meister Eckhart, all of which narrate back to him some version of what he is experiencing. These voices amount to the prattling of Job's friends, whether they tell him that God is revealing himself through "the spuming / of bile," or "how good it is to suffer // in emptiness: / *All sorrow comes from love and from holding dear.*" After trying "to hold nothing dear," and finding this to be the way of despair and loathing, the speaker like Job "gave it back to God" and surrenders himself to his own condition. In the poem's closing images, his body lies, rather like Eliot's etherized patient,

> on the hard slab
> by the half-frozen river, where the soul
> stirred weakly in an alien country . . .

If the poem ends on a note of failure, the speaker's having not achieved what he set out to do, the soul still broken and longing for its own re-integration, it is nevertheless possible to read something hopeful in that final surrender. The silence where the poem leaves off and the white space begins contains, potentially, infinite possibility, like the whirlwind out of which God speaks to Job. The poem's ending acknowledges, albeit tacitly, that possibility, that whirlwind.

After an Adoration

They don't know what to do, now they're here, leaning

on the rotted beam of a manger
bisected by light,

among oxen and asses, a carpenter's
tools, scrub

hills receding into blurred ruins.
Into each adoration, some peculiar

disillusion intrudes: always
someone in the crowd of pilgrims

averts his gaze from the Christ child
and glares accusingly outward

as though the arrival
had satisfied nothing. Only

the haloes redeem
the squalid scene: beasts'

breaths fuming in starlight,
barnfowl and peacocks flocked in the crossbeams.

One wise man's
mind has begun to go, and he stares

at some evil he believes
has followed him

the whole way, lodged now
in the shadowed rafters of this shed. Not

one of them could tell you what
all their longing

has accomplished: they're left
to stare into a wooden shack

where the cold
child whimpers and its mother

flails her arms in her sleep. After
an adoration, the shock

of how much remains
unrevealed; so awkwardly

the Magi kneel
in the pawed dirt

littered with gold, beseeching the helpless savior.

CONSOLATION

1.

In February, the soul
always contracts, cracks
into ice, opaque and fouled
by tire ruts, matted straw, spilt oil,
contaminants
seized up and contained—

You can trace, in the frozen splashes, layers of rain,
and the waste
that drifted inside:

Here in the split kingdom
of matter and spirit, the soul
doesn't recognize itself
in its natural emblems,

so I fill it in:
slash of ice from the drainpipe, anything
straining forward
but congealed—

This winter, disconsolate, I hunger for nothing,
but the quarter-moon's
so bright you can see the rest of its globe
slightly outlined
against the black, the implied circle
closed.

2.

In *Natural Theology,* William Paley
detected God's omnipotence
everywhere, even in the providential design
of the stomach, the spuming
of bile—

Everything surrendered God to him,
the story of resurrection
told and told again:
the eye "the best cure for atheism,"
membrania timpania—
microscopic bones of the ear—
revealing the intricate contrivance

of a God
bent on self-delivery
through the glorious works of his hands.

3.

I loathe each day of my life,
I will take my complaint to God—

so Job laments again, beginning
another Lent for me, in weary

February without mystery.
I walk the rough, dry woods

toward a river
crumbling the loamy banks of its gulch, ice-hatch

opening onto deep and glistening mud.
But we have to rid ourselves of the earth again,

of Job's sea "swaddled in shadows,"
of this Leviathan and serpents and beasts God made,

for Meister Eckhart threatens
"to be full of created things

is to be empty of God."
He consoles us with how good it is to suffer

in emptiness:
All sorrow comes from love and from holding dear.

This afternoon I tried to hold
nothing I could think of dear—how quickly the world shrank from my
 touch,

and I loathed the burnt pastures bared to the sun,
and the useless

scrubs and flattened rocks and and ice-flashing roofs of barns,
and all the divine effluvia I could see:

I gave it back
to God and lay myself, diminished and cold

on the hard slab
by the half-frozen river where the soul

stirred weakly in alien country, still hankering and unhealed.

Doxology

Let me laud you, God of salve and hurt,

begetter of all things
marred
and mercy-ridden—

This sprout of beggarweed, these lilac stalks
need say nothing: extolling
of scrub and vine. And even
the slackwater odor
of full gullies in drifts of sludge
attests to you—

There's nothing
the heavens haven't uttered
already in shudders
of animation more firm than words—

Flock of blackbirds over dull neon
in Thanksgiving's rainy dusk, rush
of wind through bare sweet

cherry, swelter of squirrels:
so little

abides,
so much recalls our turning
back toward you
from whom all blessings flow
endlessly away: magnificats
in the western smolder, praise
of what can't stay
unspeakable . . .

Let one
supplication cohere until I can utter it:

let what I call
out for come for me
sometimes,
and what I mean

and what it means for me,
touch—

All Saints

The demystification
unfurls. Arcana, manifestly
occult, are no more
at our disposal.
The xenotransplantation[34]
of the vatic
into vernacular
has been halted pending further
investigation. All's
serioburlesque & subcelestial.

---

34 Transplantation of nonhuman matter—cells, tissues, organs—into a human recipient

Marjorie Maddox (1959)

Marjorie Maddox is a professor of English and creative writing at Lock Haven University and the author of 11 volumes of poetry, including *Transplant, Transport, Transubstantiation*, which was a runner-up for the Brittingham and Felix Pollak Prizes, and *True, False, None of the Above*, which was an Illumination Book Award Medalist. She has a BA from Wheaton College in Illinois and an MFA from Cornell University, where she studied under A. R. Ammons and was a Sage Graduate Fellow.

Maddox, who grew up Protestant but converted to Catholicism, combines the physical and spiritual, the everyday and the extraordinary, in her work. No object or topic is off limits—body parts, news, baseball, heart surgery, ants. A discursive poet like Ammons, she often begins with an observation and progresses by comparison before returning to the opening observation, which, in turn, has been expanded or complicated. We see this, for example, in "Ash Wednesday," collected below, which begins and ends with the contrast between clean skin and the "grime of our humanness." The poem suggests that true cleanliness comes by acknowledging one's filth and warns against being "deceived into piety" that is merely external. Her book *Transplant, Transport, Transubstantiation* contains a number of response poems to poets like Robert Frost, Louise Erdrich, Gerard Manley Hopkins, Gertrude Stein, and others. The opening poem from that collection, "How Spiritual Are You?," which is a response to a quiz in *Time* magazine, is collected here. Maddox investigates in this and other poems how language can both form us into what we are and force us into what we are not.

Maddox is the winner of an Academy of American Poets Prize, the Cornell University Robert Chasen Memorial Poetry Prize, the Paumanok Poetry Award, and *Seattle Review*'s Bentley Prize. She has been awarded two fellowships to Virginia Center for the Creative Arts and currently serves as the assistant editor of *Presence: A Journal of Catholic Poetry*.

HOW SPIRITUAL ARE YOU?
—Time *magazine quiz, 10/25/04*

Tallying twenty *True* or *False*
answers to wishy-washy visions, I'm translated
from a poet of faith into
    "a practical empiricist lacking self transcendence"
according to a noted psychologist
touted as today's expert.
I don't like flunking and try again.
Any room for fudging? To insert faith? Even a seed of the spiritual?
    "extrasensory perception"?
    "completely unaware of things going on around me"?
    "I love the blooming of flowers . . . as much as seeing an old friend"?
Though I scan and re-scan, all I can check with confidence
is the final slot—the quizmaster's definition of extreme?—
    "I believe miracles happen."
A half-dozen more statements I rationalize as "sometimes,"
insulted by society's synonyms of "spiritual" and "spacey."
As a poet, I should be used to this
but gain no points from that either.
A sidebar promises to explain a "God gene"
inherent in some of us—a cultural twist on predestination
that leaves me unable to select the first square:
    "I often feel so connected to the people around me
    that it is like there is no separation between us."
Where is the "stranger in a strange land" line?
Where is the question, "Do you believe
in one God, the Father Almighty...?"

ASH WEDNESDAY

Fingernails scrubbed clean as latrines
in the army, this symbol
of a man dirties his thumb
with our skin, the powdery ash riding high
on his pores, not sinking in
before he sketches the gray
of our dirt-birth across a brow
we were born to furrow.

Listen to the sound of forgiveness:
the crossing of skin, the cult-
like queuing up to explode
in ripped whispers, "Lord,
have mercy, Lord, have
mercy, Lord, have mercy."

And we want it. And we take it
home with us to stare back
from a lover's forehead,
to come off in a smear on the sheets
as we roll onto each other's skin,
or to wear like a bindhi this medal of our not winning
each day we wake to the worlds
we are and are not.

And when we wake too early
before the light of just-becoming-day
sneaks in on us, and we stand lonely, deceived
into piety, scrubbing away the grime of our humanness
like fierce fierce toothbrushes on latrines
in the army, there it is still,
raw with our washings:
the human beneath.

Angela Alaimo O'Donnell (1960)

In her 2020 sonnet cycle *Andalusian Hours*, Angela Alaimo O'Donnell channels the voice and mind of the twentieth-century Southern Catholic fiction writer Flannery O'Connor. O'Connor also forms the subject of O'Donnell's scholarly work *Radical Ambivalence: Race in Flannery O'Connor*, published the same year as *Andalusian Hours*. Like the critically examined O'Connor of the scholarly book, the poetically imagined Flannery offers herself as the study in complexity which fallen human nature inevitably proves to be. The title, *Andalusian Hours*, implies not only the limits of time—Flannery O'Connor's brief life might have been measured in hours—but also the liturgical "hours" of monastic prayer. In these sonnets, Flannery as poetic soliloquist prays her way forward through her own illness-marked *hours* and writerly calling.

"Flannery's Manifesto" flowers from a snippet of O'Connor's own written voice, in this case a remark in a letter to a friend noting O'Connor's mother's characteristically exasperated commentary on her daughter's writing. The resulting soliloquy is a meditation on vocation, a *fiat* to the inexplicable work to which God has called, not *the writer* generically, but *this writer*, this particular "crooked heart" which nevertheless bears his image. If her mother's lack of sympathetic vision frustrates her, she is quick to acknowledge that she herself hardly understands the charism that has mastered her, except that its purpose is to make the reader "marvel that the world's still here, / that somebody watches and holds it all dear."

O'Donnell's eponymous pilgrim, meanwhile, from the 2017 collection *Still Pilgrim*, works her way through a similar liturgy of observances at the shrine of the everyday, traveling through territories of memory and contemplation even as she meets the obligations of her particular, multilayered calling: mother, daughter, lover, reader, writer, city-dweller, inhabitant of history and the traditions of art and faith. Throughout O'Donnell's work, contemporary human experience nevertheless inhabits a sacramental economy which renders time, language, and perception as movements in a liturgy, as her villanelle "For Shadowment" suggests.

Angela Alaimo O'Donnell is the author of eight books of poems and four prose works. O'Donnell, who holds degrees from Penn State University and the University of North Carolina at Chapel Hill, teaches English, creative writing, and American Catholic Studies at Fordham University.

To Be a Pilgrim

To be a pilgrim is to ring the stones
with the clean music of your best black heels,
each click a lucky strike that sparks a fire
to see by, that lights up the long and level road

you walk with no map, no stick, no wheels
to relieve you when your feet ache and tire.

To be a pilgrim own what you own,
stuff it in your clutch, lug it in your tote,
all the heavy history you'd like to lose
nestled up against your dead mother's shoes.
To be a pilgrim you must be a killer
of myth, a new invention of desire.
Every pilgrim is a truth-teller.
Every pilgrim is a liar.

FLANNERY'S MANIFESTO

*"Do you think . . . that you are really using the talent God gave you
when you don't write something that a lot, a LOT, of people like?"*
—Flannery O'Connor, quoting Regina O'Connor, April 3, 1959,
The Habit of Being

I do admire her confidence that my
gift comes from God. That it's not a game or
a trick, an affliction that she must endure.
My gospel-knowing mother fears that I
might be the fearful servant, the one who
buries his treasure in the dirty ground.
She might be right. But what else can I do
but write what my crooked heart tells me to?
I know I am a trial, hard to be around.
But what else is making fiction for
if not to trouble folks, mess with their heads,
make them question why they rise from their beds
if not to marvel that the world's still here,
that some body watches and holds it all dear.

Julia Spicher Kasdorf (1962)

Julia Spicher Kasdorf was born in Lewistown, Pennsylvania, to Mennonite parents who had left the community. She grew up outside Pittsburgh and was educated at Goshen College and New York University, where she earned a PhD. Kasdorf's poetry is direct and sensuous, drawing both from the Mennonite belief that language is "a useful, solid bucket to hold truths as clear as water" (as she wrote in her essay "Bringing Home the Work") and the liturgy and symbols of Episcopalianism. In "Mennonites," for example, which is included in this volume, she begins with simple declarative sentences:

> We keep our quilts in closets and do not dance.
> We hoe thistles along fence rows for fear
> we may not be perfect as our Heavenly Father.
> We clean up his disasters . . .

As the poem progresses, and descriptions of Mennonite martyrs are added, it becomes a kind of confession of faith before ending elegiacally: "We do not drink; we sing. Unaccompanied on Sundays, / those hymns in four parts, our voices lift with such force / that we lift, as chaff lifts toward God."

Kasdorf is preoccupied with borders in her work—between the past and the present, the sacred and the secular, and the spirit and the body. In her first volume of poetry, *Sleeping Preacher*, she mixes memories of Amish uncles and the Mennonite women with scenes of modern life in a multicultural New York City to make distinctions and locate similarities. Religious communities give "life coherence," Kasdorf tells Anya Krugovoy Silver in an interview for *Image*, but they also provide members with a space into which they can welcome outsiders. At the same time, such boundaries can contribute to violence against others. "Maybe one root of violence," she remarks, "is the stifled desire to transcend one's own community or its identity-building memory and connect with others."

Kasdorf is the author of four books of poetry: *Sleeping Preacher, Eve's Striptease, Poetry in America*, and *Shale Play: Poems and Photographs from the Fracking Fields*. She won the Agnes Lynch Starrett Poetry Prize for *Sleeping Preacher* and received the Book of the Year award from the Conference on Christianity and Literature for her collection of essays, *The Body and the Book: Writing from a Mennonite Life*. The recipient of a Pushcart Prize and a National Endowment for the Arts Fellowship in Poetry, Kasdorf is currently the Liberal Arts Professor of English at Penn State University.

DYING WITH AMISH UNCLES

The ground was frozen so hard
his sons used a jackhammer to pry
open a grave in the rocky field
where Grossdaadi's wife and daughter
lay under the streaked stones
that tell only last names:
Yoder, Zook, Yoder.

Amish uncles, Grossdaadi's sons,
shoveled earth on the box;
stones clattered on wood then quieted
while we sang hymns to the wind.
Bending over the hole,
Uncle Kore wouldn't wipe
his dripping nose and chin.

Ten years later when we gather
for July ham and moon pies,
the uncles stand to sing
Grossdaadi's favorite hymns.
At "*Gott ist die Liebe*,"[35]
they almost laugh
with the tears running
into their beards;
Abe and Mose and Ben
do not wipe them.

Their voices come deep as graves
and unashamed of shirtsleeves
or suspenders. Seeing them cry
that brave, I think the uncles
mustn't die, that they'll stay
with those of us who must,
being so much better than we are
at weathering death.

---

35 "God is love"

MENNONITES

We keep our quilts in closets and do not dance.
We hoe thistles along fence rows for fear
we may not be perfect as our Heavenly Father.
We clean up his disasters. No one has to
call; we just show up in the wake of tornadoes
with hammers, after floods with buckets.
Like Jesus, the servant, we wash each other's feet
twice a year and eat the Lord's Supper,
afraid of sins hidden so deep in our organs
they could damn us unawares,
swallowing this bread, his body, this juice.
Growing up, we love the engravings in *Martyrs Mirror*:
men drowned like cats in burlap sacks,
the Catholic inquisitors,
the woman who handed a pear to her son,
her tongue screwed to the roof of her mouth
to keep her from singing hymns while she burned.
We love Catherine the Great and the rich tracts
she gave us in the Ukraine, bright green winter wheat,
the Cossacks who torched it, and Stalin,
who starved our cousins while wheat rotted
in granaries. We must love our enemies.
We must forgive as our sins are forgiven,
our great-uncle tells us, showing the chain
and ball in a cage whittled from one block of wood
while he was in prison for refusing to shoulder
a gun. He shows the clipping from 1916:
Mennonites are German milksops, too yellow to fight.
We love those Nazi soldiers who, like Moses,
led the last cattle cars rocking out of the Ukraine,
crammed with our parents—children then—
learning the names of Kansas, Saskatchewan, Paraguay.
This is why we cannot leave the beliefs
or what else would we be? why we eat
'til we're drunk on shoofly and moon pies and borscht.
We do not drink; we sing. Unaccompanied on Sundays,

those hymns in four parts, our voices lift with such force
that we lift, as chaff lifts toward God.

A PASS

Forgive us our trespasses
as we forgive, I softly recite

among strangers, remembering
the hand of an older man

gliding up my thin dress.
I twist free of him,

keep speaking as if he is just
a rich family friend chatting,

and I am still safe
in the shape of my skin.

Of course, it sets me back,
as each death resurrects

the memory of all other deaths,
and you must return to mourn

your full store of passings afresh.
A child cannot be accused

of seducing a neighbor man,
but as the girl grows, the bones

of her cheeks and pelvis jut
like blades beneath her skin,

gorgeous weapons of revenge.
At last, the lusts of *those*

who trespass against us bear
some resemblance to our own:

shame and rage, heavy as coins
sewn in the lining of an exile's coat.

When an immigrant ship went down
in Lake Erie, passengers who refused

to shed their heavy garments
drowned, yards from shore.

THE KNOWLEDGE OF GOOD AND EVIL

When beautiful Snow White bit and swooned
on the dwarfs' cottage stoop, pale bosom heaving,
and a chuckling crone scooted off with her basket
of ruby apples, I shrieked, kicking theater seats.
No hushing would stop me, so I was dragged across
strangers' knees, up a dark, inclined aisle, over
the lobby's red carpet, past ushers sharing smirks
with a candy case lady, out onto the sidewalk
which was just there on Clay Avenue in Jeannette,
Pennsylvania. The glassworks was still going
and Gillespie's still sent receipts in pneumatic tubes
when you bought a slip or new pair of shoes. Only then
I stopped screaming and grasped my shuddering breath,
blinking at parking meters, grateful it was still light
outside that story, which was worse than disobedience
or the snake I saw slithering beyond the frame
of my Bible story page. I'd studied Adam's face
and Eve, who tempted him, hair hiding her breasts
as they walked in that exotic garden, already bent
over with guilt, palm fronds at their waists.
Mom coaxed me back to the lobby, and I hovered
in buttery light by the popcorn machine. The prince
returns! She comes back to life! Go in and see!
she crooned with the ushers, but I refused. Even when
they pushed me toward a crack in the dark double doors
and I glimpsed a prince and lavish wedding dress,
I could not believe she was alive and happy ever after.

I was a heretic too insulted by the cross
to accept resurrection. I knew that marriage
is just a trick cooked up by the grownups
to keep me from screaming my head off.

Christian Wiman (1966)

Christian Wiman writes a poetry of seeking. In a 2007 essay, "Looking Into the Abyss," which chronicles the poet's unexpected reawakening to Christian faith, Wiman describes the human condition in terms of separation: never "quite at home in your life," always conscious of distance between the lonely, fallen self and the "divinity" for which that self longs. Wiman's engagement with questions of faith presumes that the believer and the unbeliever are in essence the same person. The "completely modern" person, to borrow Wiman's own phrasing, nevertheless bears in himself a "strong spiritual hunger," too often inchoate and unacknowledged because the modern "consciousness" lacks any language for articulating the real object of its longing. Wiman's poetic project, then, is to render that longing, that seeking, into a common language in which the believer and the unbeliever might converse with each other—in which, too, the believer or the unbeliever might converse with the other in himself.

Wiman's poetry evinces a fluid facility with rhyme and meter, though he moves easily between traditional form and free verse. Rejecting neither form nor the loosening of form, on the level of poetics, too, he is what he has characterized as an "unbelieving believer," the one always identifying with its other as though seeking to heal some perceived breach between them. Likewise, Wiman's poetic voice, even in the space of a single poem, can travel an entire range from ironic jokiness to psalmist's lament. "All My Friends Are Finding New Beliefs," from Wiman's 2020 collection, *Survival Is a Style*, exemplifies this tonal range, as well as a level of control over line and syntax that provides, for free verse, the kind of subtext that the tensions of a traditional form can generate. Beginning with a tongue-in-cheek, almost mocking catalog of various observed enthusiasms—"Catholicism," "trees," "Paleo, Keto, South Beach, Bourbon"—midway in its life's journey the poem unravels into lamentation, an unraveling signaled by the disintegration of its syntax. The poem ends on a fragment—"and my friends, my beautiful, credible friends"—in which the speaker, who has talked himself out of his own ironic distance, reveals his longing to believe, as his friends do, in *something*. Belief, initially a thing to joke about, has become instead, in itself, an object of desire.

Born in 1966 in Snyder, Texas, Christian Wiman is a graduate of Washington and Lee University and has taught at Northwestern University, Stanford University, Lynchburg College, the Prague School of Economics, Yale University, and the Yale Institute for Sacred Music. He served as editor of *Poetry* magazine from 2003 to 2013. His first book, *The Long Home*, received the Nicholas Roerich Prize from Story Line Press. He is the author subsequently of seven books of poetry and four collections of essays dealing with poetics, with questions of religious faith, and with the problem of human suffering, rooted in the poet's own experience of living with a terminal cancer diagnosis. His honors include a Guggenheim Fellowship, a National Book Critics Circle Award, and the Aiken Taylor Award for Modern American Poetry.

AFTER THE DIAGNOSIS

No remembering now
when the apple sapling was blown
almost out of the ground.
No telling how,
with all the other trees around,
it alone was struck.
It must have been luck,
he thought for years, so close
to the house it grew.
It must have been night.
Change is a thing one sleeps through
when young, and he was young.
If there was a weakness in the earth,
a give he went down on his knees
to find and feel the limits of,
there is no longer.
If there was one random blow from above
the way he's come to know
from years in this place,
the roots were stronger.
Whatever the case,
he has watched this tree survive
wind ripping at his roof for nights
on end, heats and blights
that left little else alive.
No remembering now...
A day's changes mean all to him
and all days come down
to one clear pane
through which he sees
among all the other trees
this leaning, clenched, unyielding one
that seems cast
in the form of a blast
that would have killed it,
as if something at the heart of things,

and with the heart of things,
had willed it.

LORD IS NOT A WORD

Lord is not a word.
Song is not a salve.
Suffer the child, who lived
on sunlight and solitude.
Savor the man, craving
earth like an aftertaste.
To discover in one's hand
two local stones the size
of a dead man's eyes
saves no one, but to fling them
with a grace you did not know
you knew, to bring them
skimming homing
over blue, is to discover
the river from which they came.
Mild merciful amnesia
through which I've moved
as through a blue atmosphere
of almost and was,
how is it now,
like ruins unearthed by ruin,
my childhood should rise?
Lord, suffer me to sing
these wounds by which I am made
and marred, savor this creature
whose aloneness you ease and are.

PRAYER

For all
the pain

passed down
the genes

or latent
in the very grain

of being;
for the lordless

mornings,
the smear

of spirit
words intuit

and inter;
for all

the nightfall
neverness

inking
into me

even now,
my prayer

is that a mind
blurred

by anxiety
or despair

might find
here

a trace
of peace.

THE PREACHER ADDRESSES THE SEMINARIANS

I tell you it's a bitch existence some Sundays
and it's no good pretending you don't have to pretend,

don't have to hitch up those gluefutured nags Hope and Help
and whip the sorry chariot of yourself

toward whatever hell your heaven is on days like these.
I tell you it takes some hunger heaven itself won't slake

to be so twitchingly intent on the pretty organist's pedaling,
so lizardly alert to the curvelessness of her choir robe.

Here it comes, brothers and sisters, the confession of sins,
hominy hominy, dipstick doxology, one more churchcurdled hymn

we don't so much sing as haunt: grounded altos, gear-grinding tenors,
two score and ten gently bewildered men lip-synching along.

You're up, Pastor. Bring on the unthunder. Some trickle-piss tangent
to reality. Some bit of the Gospel grueling out of you.

I tell you sometimes mercy means nothing
but release from this homiletic hologram, a little fleshstep

sideways, as it were, setting passion on autopilot (as if it weren't!)
to gaze out in peace at your peaceless parishioners:

boozeglazes and facelifts, bad mortgages, bored marriages,
a masonry of faces at once specific and generic,

and here and there that rapt famished look that leaps
from person to person, year to year, like a holy flu.

All these little crevices into which you've crawled
like a chubby plumber with useless tools:

Here, have a verse for your wife's death.
Here, have a death for your life's curse.

I tell you some Sundays even the children's sermon
—maybe especially this—sharks your gut

like a bite of tin some beer-guzzling goat
either drunkenly or mistakenly decides to sample.

I know what you're thinking. Christ's in this.
He'll get to it, the old cunner, somewhere somehow

there's the miracle meat, the aurora borealis blood,
every last atom compacted to a grave

and the one thing that every man must lose to save.
Well, friends, I'm here to tell you two things today.

First, though this is not, for me, one of those bilious abrading days,
though in fact I stand before you in a rage of faith

and have all good hope that you will all go help
untold souls back into their bodies,

ease the annihilating No above which they float,
the truth is our only savior is failure.

Which brings me to the second thing: that goat.
It was real. It is, as is usually the case, the displacement of agency

that is the lie. It was long ago, Mexico, my demon days:
It was a wager whose stakes I failed to appreciate.

He tottered. He flowered. He writhed time to a fraught quiet,
and kicked occasionally, and lay there twitching, watching me die.

PROLOGUE

Church or sermon, prayer or poem:
the failure of religious feeling is a form.

*

The failure of religious feeling is a form
of love that, though it could not survive

the cataclysmic joy of its inception,
nevertheless preserves its own sane something,

a space in which the grievers gather,
inviolate ice that the believers weather:

church or sermon, prayer or poem.

*

Finer and finer the meaningless distinctions:
theodicies, idiolects, books, books, books.

I need a space for unbelief to breathe.
I need a form for failure, since it is what I have.

ALL MY FRIENDS ARE FINDING NEW BELIEFS

All my friends are finding new beliefs.
This one converts to Catholicism and this one to trees.
In a highly literary and hitherto religiously-indifferent Jew
God whomps on like a genetic generator.
Paleo, Keto, Zone, South Beach, Bourbon.
Exercise regimens so extreme she merges with machine.
One man marries a woman twenty years younger
and twice in one brunch uses the word verdant;
another's brick-fisted belligerence gentles
into dementia, and one, after a decade of finical feints and teases
like a sandpiper at the edge of the sea,
decides to die.

Priesthoods and beasthoods, sombers and glees,
high-styled renunciations and avocations of dirt,
sobrieties, satieties, pilgrimages to the very bowels of being...
All my friends are finding new beliefs
and I am finding it harder and harder to keep track
of the new gods and the new loves,
and the old gods and the old loves,
and the days have daggers, and the mirrors motives,
and the planet's turning faster and faster in the blackness,
and my nights, and my doubts, and my friends,
my beautiful, credible friends.

Even Bees Know What Zero Is

That's enough memories, thank you, I'm stuffed.
I'll need a memory vomitorium if this goes on.
How much attention can one man have?
Which reminds me: once I let the gas go on flowing
after my car was full and watched it spill its smell
(and potential hell) all over the ground around me.
I had to pay for that, and in currency quite other than attention.
I've had my fill of truth, too, come to think of it.
It's all smeary in me, I'm like a waterlogged Bible:
enough with the aborted prophecies and garbled laws,
ancient texts holey as a teen's jeans, begone begats!
Live long enough, and you can't tell what's resignation, what resolve.
That's the bad news. The good news? You don't give a shit.
My life. It's like a library that closes for a long, long time
—a *lifetime*, some of the disgrunts mutter—
and when it opens opens only to an improved confusion:
theology where poetry should be, psychology crammed with math.
And I'm all the regulars searching for their sections
and I'm the detonated disciplines too.
But most of all I'm the squat, smocked, bingo-winged woman
growing more granitic and less placable by the hour
as citizen after citizen blurts some version of
"What the hell!" or "I thought you'd all died!"

and the little stamp she stamps on the flyleaf
to tell you when your next generic mystery is due
that thing goes stamp right on my very soul.
Which is one more thing I'm done with, by the way,
the whole concept of soul. Even bees know what zero is,
scientists have learned, which means bees know my soul.
I'm done, I tell you, I'm due, I'm Oblivion's datebook.
I'm a sunburned earthworm, a mongoose's milk tooth,
a pleasure tariff, yesterday's headcheese, spiritual gristle.
I'm the Apocalypse's popsicle. I'm a licked Christian.

John Poch (1966)

John Poch's work is marked by a formal subtlety and a broad linguistic palate. A Poch poem might begin with a few lines from a John Mellencamp song, dancing Dallas Cowboy cheerleaders, an afternoon of shooting feral hogs from a helicopter with an AR-15, or a description of Dante's tomb. Taut but opulent lines make his poems seem both "fast" and "slow." The iambic pentameter of "Et Cetera," for example, pushes the pace forward while Poch's striking similes—"stars that looked like salt"—pull it back:

> From town you walked home lit, and laughing, pulled
> me out of bed for stars that looked like salt
> or holes of light in black or jewels to you.
> You took my hand and drug me to the roof
> to understand the heavens come so close.

The poem ends, like many of Poch's poems, with a turn that is syntactically rich: "We kissed . . . Your mouth was sweet / and made me sick in love with our defeat."

An active Presbyterian, Poch writes poetry that is also marked by a profound understanding of God's grace, a wry sense of humor, and a mischievous intelligence. In "Good God," for example, a poem on the fall of Adam, the speaker wonders what he would have done in Adam's place: "By candle light I wax self-referential. / I mind my manners, modesty, and swell, / ridiculous as fig leaves, confidential," and thus becomes guilty of Adam's original pride in the very moment he thinks he would have avoided it. "Why do I do the same old raising hell," the speaker wonders, conscience pricked, before concluding, "Here comes the cancer and the prison cell. / Life is knowing dying as essential." Collected in this volume are Poch's poems "Prayer" and "Ignored Woodwork in Old Churches." In the latter, the spiritual hunger of the trout in "Christian Anger" is figured as wood worms boring into a monk's seat: "Softer than fetus flesh, / each worm extended the finger of its hunger, / and like a nearly imperceptible symbol of / a crucifixion nail, drove its being / into boring."

Poch is a professor of creative writing at Texas Tech University and the author of six books of poetry, including *Fix Quiet*, which won the 2014 New Criterion Poetry Prize, and *Two Men Fighting with a Knife*, which won the Donald Justice Award. Also a winner of the 1998 "Discovery"/The Nation Prize, Poch was the inaugural Colgate University Creative Writing Fellow from 2000 to 2001 and was a founding editor of the magazine *32 Poems*.

PRAYER

Invisible One,
when I close my eyes
I can see you
in another way
like part of a Pollock[36]
I can make sense of
not because I see
a figure or a face
but because the love
of a moving brush
slung over wet gesso
tired of a life of air
proves much.
Things are not things.
Time is not time.
Love is not love.
But prayer is a thread in air
between. A wire clear
oil trickles down
as slow as light at noon
and young hunger.
Angels, please turn my words
like bees make flowers
into honey and wax
and a form for genesis.

---

36 Jackson Pollock was an abstract expressionist painter.

IGNORED WOODWORK IN OLD CHURCHES

Outside the intertwining diamond rings
on a saint's dress in a painting, beyond the frame
next to the chapel where the guidebook
mistook Dante's hell for purgatory,
his suicidal Harpies for Man-Doves,
just past the Brunelleschi crucifix,
the seats where the preaching friars sit
are carved with scrolls and heads of animals
or men or monsters in between.
I want to know what kind of wood
and how the hinges will convert the seat
into a stall where a monk can stand for a while
to worship, tucked neatly into his niche
like the saint he is or may become.
Look closely on the armrest and you see
the pinprick wormholes perpetrated
over centuries. Softer than fetus flesh,
each worm extended the finger of its hunger,
and like a nearly imperceptible symbol of
a crucifixion nail, drove its being
into boring. Almost no one notices
in this nave where the naïve are drawn
like moths to where the stained glass
light above a chapel altar seems to make
each of us a cracking chrysalis restored
to what we always must have been becoming.

Jennifer Reeser (1968)

Born in 1968 in Lake Charles, Louisiana, Jennifer Reeser draws on a literary and cultural heritage that includes, on the one hand, Robert Frost, and on the other, such indigenous American peoples as the Powhatan and the Cherokee, who comprise her ancestry. In her writing, Reeser fuses the long formal tradition of English and European poetry with the concerns and conventions of Native American prayer, song, and ritual. She is the author of four books of poetry and a translator not only from the French and Russian—particularly the poems of Anna Akhmatova—but also from the Cherokee and various other indigenous American languages.

A practicing Christian, yet aware of the cultural depredations wrought in the name of Christianity, Reeser the translator enters with sensitivity into the ritual prayers and songs of Native peoples, rendering them in the rhyme and meter of traditional poetry in English, and a heightened, almost stylized formal language, all of which, as she has asserted, underscore the highly controlled, formalized settings of the originals. The result is a paradoxical cultural fusion: the European form which is ultimately most true to, and best serves, the indigenous original.

Meanwhile, her own poems turn on the same integrated sense of identity: genetic, cultural, religious. In "Nature Does Not Care," the speaker positions herself on the sidelines of Native culture, even as "our umbilical is real." Its ceremonial dances and chants extend themselves as a birthright, yet she, Christian and at least partly alien, forbears to "interrupt" them with questions, correctives, or attempts to proselytize. Instead, she chooses to remain "elusive," allied with a larger natural law that, defying cultural convention, does not turn on "what we believe / . . . nor how we feel," but on something external, objectively true.

Likewise, "O Great Spirit," a prayer-sonnet, names the Persons of the Holy Trinity. At the same time, it associates those names not only with traditional Native terms, but also with known, loved people and belongings still inhabited by the memory of those lives. The poem ends by conflating the Apostle Paul's "cloud of witnesses," the Communion of Saints in heaven, with the "dark people" of the poet's past, who also witness her work in the present. Here again, Reeser's particular poetics of identity reveals itself: a poetics that places disparate traditions in a relationship of mutual conversation and service, the one not silencing, but amplifying, the other.

NATURE DOES NOT CARE

Nature does not care what we believe,
By what way we were formed, nor how we feel.
Look in my face, blood brother, see and grieve
Or joy, that our umbilical is real.
I shall not draw you from the powwow dance.
I will not bore with silly inquiries,
Nor interrupt the ceremonial chants
Through which you thrill the pretty, British tease.
Off, in the shadows, half lit, unobtrusive
I shall remain, a sister to the smoke,
With changing features—childlike and elusive,
With chalky power you may not invoke.
I will not ask you how, nor what it means.
The answer is not learned, but in my genes.

O GREAT SPIRIT

Great Spirit of the God who is alive,
Whose risen Son I seek before the dawn,
Who makes the black and gold sunflower thrive,
The earthworm loosen soil beneath the lawn;
Great Spirit, grant my great-grandmother's looks
Attend me while I rub her cherry hutch.
Great Spirit, grant my late grandfather's books
Preserve his signature I love to touch.
Surround and show to me to that massive cloud
Of witnesses—undauntable or docile.
Allow their countenances to enshroud
My shoulders, spoken of by Your Apostle.
Send generous *Nunnehi*[37] to my steeple,
Returning me, at last, to my dark people.

---

37 Spirit-people in Cherokee mythology. The Cherokee word has been translated variously as "The People Who Live Anywhere," or as "The People Who Live Forever."

Tracy K. Smith (1972)

In her memoir, *Ordinary Light*, Tracy K. Smith recalls the moment in a college Bible study, her freshman year at Harvard, in which she attempts to phrase a question about God: "Maybe there's something in all this that nobody's named before. Something . . . better." Smith, who served as US Poet Laureate from 2017–2019, seeks not so much to name that "something . . . that nobody's named before," as to establish boundaries outside which the mystery of God, the "something better," resides: unknowable, though it also suffuses, in one way or another, what the human mind can apprehend within those boundaries.

Born in 1972 in Massachusetts, the daughter of a teacher and an engineer whose work on the Hubble Telescope provides a center for some of her exploratory poems, Smith spent her California childhood in a family culture shaped by her father's scientific work and her mother's intense Christian faith. As Smith has noted, in a 2016 interview with Paul Holdengraber, "God was a presence in her life and our life, because she instilled that," though in her poems, this "instilled" presence becomes something to distill through the application, as she has put it, of "scientific law (rather than religious law)."

Neither a scientist nor a theologian, Smith has—in a wide-ranging 2011 conversation with the *Rumpus Book Club*—described her poetic process as a means for making difficult ideas "stick." The poems in her Pulitzer-Prize-winning collection *Life on Mars*, for example, probe the outer reaches of space with the Hubble Telescope even as they work through personal grief. These poems invoke questions common to both quantum physics and theology: questions about origins, about limits, about the nature of reality. "My God, It's Full of Stars" ends with the Hubble Telescope, an image at first blurred, then coming into focus. "We saw to the edge of all there is—," says her speaker, "So brutal and alive it seemed to comprehend us back." In this poem's closing lines, as the great mechanized optic nerve of the telescope makes visible the back corner of the universe, what the seers experience is something like the glory of the Lord passing Moses, hidden in the cleft of the rock, lest that glory, "brutal and alive" in its comprehension, strike him dead.

Other poems in the same collection take up this motif of seeking, while deliberately setting aside any preconceived idea of what the seeker hopes to find. In "Cathedral Kitsch," an observer, watching women light candles and pray their rosaries in the gold-leafed darkness, perceives in that atmosphere not the achievement of the divine, but of the human: "I feel / Man here. The same wish / That named the planets." Thomas Aquinas might say that all human invention is a function of man's createdness, the way in which man is most like God; in "Cathedral Kitsch," this likeness becomes a function of man's wishful thinking, that there is something beyond himself which he is nevertheless *like*. At the same time, what there is, the world itself, is inescapably sacramental, with a music heard in the cathedral's organ pipes and in "the chorus of crushed cans / Someone drags over cobbles / In the secular street." *Secular* in the poem's closing line is an interesting choice of modifiers: though typically associated with religion as its opposite, the word in its Latin origins simply means *world,* encompassing both church and street, a place where God either is or is not. If God is, then he inhabits the church, whose man-made beauty both reflects and aspires to his glory, which is never limited to or utterly defined by that space.

In still other poems, particularly those in her 2018 collection *Wade in the Water,* Smith concerns herself with God's action in a fallen world, and with human responses to the possibility of such action. The book's title poem, "Wade in the Water," derives both its title and its subject from the African-American slave experience; "Wade in the Water" is the slave spiritual—performed as a call-and-response "ring shout"—invoking the Hebrews' escape through the Red Sea as a figure for the African slave's hope for deliverance, a scriptural underwriting of the righteousness of that hope. Throughout the poem, a woman, a member of the Geechee Gullah Ring Shouters performing group, moves through an audience of strangers, telling each one, "I love you." This greeting acts as a sort of pulse in the poem, or the passing of a torch, one surviving descendant of slavery to another. It is that recurring utterance which the poem affirms in the chains of the slave's experience and in the terrifying flight to freedom, the love that is, paradoxically, "the trouble you promised." That love, born of suffering, becomes—with the re-enacted memory of suffering, in a pattern like the story of salvation itself—a legacy which the poem's speaker receives, both heritage and epiphany.

In a smaller, more immediately personal scenario, meanwhile, a shopper in the Garden of Eden organic market drops a trail of "beluga lentils" behind her: a Hansel-and-Gretel moment in which the speaker, on her way out of a world which at least presents itself as unfallen, its luxury made "desolate" by knowledge of the fallen world outside, drops a trail that leads back to the safety of the bulk-item bins. To confront the world outside, after the glossiness of the market, is a violence. Its reality "slam[s] me in the face." Yet even as the sun sets on that world, a new epoch is opening: "the dawning century." "In the end," as T. S. Eliot writes in the *Four Quartets,* "is our beginning." In the poems of Tracy K. Smith, despair and hope stand together at the threshold of a broken world that displays its wounds, even as it is being made new.

CATHEDRAL KITSCH

Does God love gold?
Does he shine back
At himself from walls
Like these, leafed
In the world's softest wealth?

Women light candles,
Pray into their fistful of beads.
Cameras spit human light
Into the vast holy dark,

And what glistens back
Is high up and cold. I feel
Man here. The same wish
That named the planets.

Man with his shoes and tools,
His insistence to prove we exist
Just like God, in the large
And the small, the great

And the frayed. In the chords
That rise from the tall brass pipes
And the chorus of crushed cans
Someone drags over cobbles
In the secular street.

My God, It's Full of Stars

1.

We like to think of it as parallel to what we know,
Only bigger. One man against the authorities.
Or one man against a city of zombies. One man

Who is not, in fact, a man, sent to understand
The caravan of men now chasing him like red ants
Let loose down the pants of America. Man on the run.

Man with a ship to catch, a payload to drop,
This message going out to all of space. . . . Though
Maybe it's more like life below the sea: silent,

Buoyant, bizarrely benign. Relics
Of an outmoded design. Some like to imagine
A cosmic mother watching through a spray of stars,

Mouthing *yes, yes* as we toddle toward the light,
Biting her lip if we teeter at some ledge. Longing
To sweep us to her breast, she hopes for the best

While the father storms through adjacent rooms
Ranting with the force of Kingdom Come,
Not caring anymore what might snap us in its jaw.

Sometimes, what I see is a library in a rural community.
All the tall shelves in the big open room. And the pencils
In a cup at Circulation, gnawed on by the entire population.

The books have lived here all along, belonging
For weeks at a time to one or another in the brief sequence
Of family names, speaking (at night mostly) to a face,

A pair of eyes. The most remarkable lies.

2.

Charlton Heston is waiting to be let in. He asked once politely.
A second time with force from the diaphragm. The third time,
He did it like Moses: arms raised high, face an apocryphal white.

Shirt crisp, suit trim, he stoops a little coming in,
Then grows tall. He scans the room. He stands until I gesture,
Then he sits. Birds commence their evening chatter. Someone fires

Charcoals out below. He'll take a whiskey if I have it. Water if I don't.
I ask him to start from the beginning, but he goes only halfway back.
That was the future once, he says. *Before the world went upside down.*

Hero, survivor, God's right hand man, I know he sees the blank
Surface of the moon where I see a language built from brick and bone.
He sits straight in his seat, takes a long, slow high-thespian breath,

Then lets it go. *For all I know, I was the last true man on this earth.* And:
May I smoke? The voices outside soften. Planes jet past heading off or back.
Someone cries that she does not want to go to bed. Footsteps overhead.

A fountain in the neighbor's yard babbles to itself, and the night air
Lifts the sound indoors. *It was another time*, he says, picking up again.
We were pioneers. Will you fight to stay alive here, riding the earth

Toward God-knows-where? I think of Atlantis buried under ice, gone
One day from sight, the shore from which it rose now glacial and stark.
Our eyes adjust to the dark.

3.

Perhaps the great error is believing we're alone,

That the others have come and gone—a momentary blip—

When all along, space might be choc-full of traffic,

Bursting at the seams with energy we neither feel

Nor see, flush against us, living, dying, deciding,

Setting solid feet down on planets everywhere,

Bowing to the great stars that command, pitching stones

At whatever are their moons. They live wondering

If they are the only ones, knowing only the wish to know,

And the great black distance they—we—flicker in.

Maybe the dead know, their eyes widening at last,

Seeing the high beams of a million galaxies flick on

At twilight. Hearing the engines flare, the horns

Not letting up, the frenzy of being. I want to be

One notch below bedlam, like a radio without a dial.

Wide open, so everything floods in at once.

And sealed tight, so nothing escapes. Not even time,

Which should curl in on itself and loop around like smoke.

So that I might be sitting now beside my father

As he raises a lit match to the bowl of his pipe

For the first time in the winter of 1959.

    4.

In those last scenes of Kubrick's *2001*
When Dave is whisked into the center of space,
Which unfurls in an aurora of orgasmic light
Before opening wide, like a jungle orchid
For a love-struck bee, then goes liquid,
Paint-in-water, and then gauze wafting out and off,
Before, finally, the night tide, luminescent
And vague, swirls in, and on and on. . . .

In those last scenes, as he floats
Above Jupiter's vast canyons and seas,
Over the lava strewn plains and mountains
Packed in ice, that whole time, he doesn't blink.
In his little ship, blind to what he rides, whisked
Across the wide-screen of unparcelled time,
Who knows what blazes through his mind?
Is it still his life he moves through, or does
That end at the end of what he can name?

On set, it's shot after shot till Kubrick is happy,
Then the costumes go back on their racks
And the great gleaming set goes black.

    5.

When my father worked on the Hubble Telescope, he said
They operated like surgeons: scrubbed and sheathed
In papery green, the room a clean cold, a bright white.

He'd read Larry Niven at home, and drink scotch on the rocks,
His eyes exhausted and pink. These were the Reagan years,
When we lived with our finger on The Button and struggled

To view our enemies as children. My father spent whole seasons
Bowing before the oracle-eye, hungry for what it would find.
His face lit-up whenever anyone asked, and his arms would rise

As if he were weightless, perfectly at ease in the never-ending
Night of space. On the ground, we tied postcards to balloons
For peace. Prince Charles married Lady Di. Rock Hudson died.

We learned new words for things. The decade changed.

The first few pictures came back blurred, and I felt ashamed
For all the cheerful engineers, my father and his tribe. The second time,
The optics jibed. We saw to the edge of all there is—

So brutal and alive it seemed to comprehend us back.

The Universe as Primal Scream

5pm on the nose. They open their mouths
And it rolls out: high, shrill and metallic.
First the boy, then his sister. Occasionally,
They both let loose at once, and I think
Of putting on my shoes to go up and see
Whether it is merely an experiment
Their parents have been conducting
Upon the good crystal, which must surely
Lie shattered to dust on the floor.

Maybe the mother is still proud
Of the four pink lungs she nursed
To such might. Perhaps, if they hit
The magic decibel, the whole building
Will lift-off, and we'll ride to glory
Like Elijah. If this is it—if this is what
Their cries are cocked toward—let the sky
Pass from blue, to red, to molten gold,
To black. Let the heaven we inherit approach.

Whether it is our dead in Old Testament robes,
Or a door opening onto the roiling infinity of space.
Whether it will bend down to greet us like a father,
Or swallow us like a furnace. I'm ready
To meet what refuses to let us keep anything
For long. What teases us with blessings,
Bends us with grief. Wizard, thief, the great
Wind rushing to knock our mirrors to the floor,
To sweep our short lives clean. How mean

Our racket seems beside it. My stereo on shuffle.
The neighbor chopping onions through a wall.
All of it just a hiccough against what may never
Come for us. And the kids upstairs still at it,
Screaming like the Dawn of Man, as if something
They have no name for has begun to insist
Upon being born.

WADE IN THE WATER
for the Geechee Gullah Ring Shouters

One of the women greeted me.
I love you, she said. She didn't
Know me, but I believed her,
And a terrible new ache
Rolled over in my chest,
Like in a room where the drapes
Have been swept back. I love you,
I love you, as she continued
Down the hall past other strangers,
Each feeling pierced suddenly
By pillars of heavy light.
I love you, throughout
The performance, in every
Handclap, every stomp.
I love you in the rusted iron
Chains someone was made
To drag until love let them be
Unclasped and left empty
In the center of the ring.
I love you in the water
Where they pretended to wade,
Singing that old blood-deep song
That dragged us to those banks
And cast us in. I love you,
The angles of it scraping at
Each throat, shouldering past
The swirling dust motes
In those beams of light
That whatever we now knew
We could let ourselves feel, knew
To climb. O Woods—O Dogs—
O Tree—O Gun—O *Girl, run*—
O Miraculous Many Gone—
O Lord—O Lord—O Lord—
Is this love the trouble you promised?

THE GARDEN OF EDEN

What a profound longing
I feel, just this very instant,
For the Garden of Eden
On Montague Street
Where I seldom shopped,
Usually only after therapy
Elbow sore at the crook
From a handbasket filled
To capacity. The glossy pastries!
Pomegranate, persimmon, quince!
Once, a bag of black beluga
Lentils spilt a trail behind me
While I labored to find
A tea they refused to carry.
It was Brooklyn. My thirties.
Everyone I knew was living
The same desolate luxury,
Each ashamed of the same things:
Innocence and privacy. I'd lug
Home the paper bags, doing
Bank-balance math and counting days.
I'd squint into it, or close my eyes
And let it slam me in the face—
The known sun setting
On the dawning century.

Tania Runyan (1972)

"I came face to face with Jesus Christ while watching the *Phil Donahue Show*," Tania Runyan writes in the foreword to her fifth collection of poetry, *What Will Soon Take Place*. She was a freshman in high school at the time and Donahue was interviewing Elizabeth Clare Prophet, the founder of the cult that claimed a nuclear attack from Russia would soon end the world. Runyan, suddenly gripped by a fear, turns to Christ with the help of her older sister and makes a profession of faith. While her theology has changed over the years, her faith hasn't. Many of her poems are overtly theological, written in response to biblical texts or in the voice of biblical characters. *What Will Soon Take Place*, for example, addresses contemporary Evangelical notions of the apocalypse. "Revelation," Runyan writes, "isn't about preparing for tomorrow's apocalypse, but clinging to God today, drawing near to him amidst dangers." Her previous collection, *Second Sky*, investigates both Paul's theology and person while, at the same time, offering a kind of translation—in contemporary imagery and diction—of his teaching. Her third collection, *A Thousand Vessels*, contains only poems written from the perspective of various women in the Bible.

Writing poems so closely tied to the biblical text is full of pitfalls. It risks a poem's ontological integrity. It risks the poet's imaginative freedom, potentially pitting it against faithfulness, as well as the poet's linguistic inventiveness. Runyan avoids these pitfalls with sure-footedness. Her poetry is fresh, perverse in its orthodoxy, and belonging entirely to itself while also pointing us elsewhere. Revelation, Runyan writes, "Will not rush through your heart like a ball lightning" in "Things That Will Soon Take Place." Rather, it will burrow "inside you like a tick": "Soon you will see / seraph wings in the price tags, / hear trumpets in the vents." In "The Fruit of the Spirit," a mother is comforted by the voice of Christ who commends her for refraining from eating Cherry Garcia ice cream for ten hours and not swearing at her kids: "That's as sweet / as peaches in August, my friend, / that's juice running down my beard."

Runyan is the author of four guides to writing and five volumes of poetry. Her first collection, *Delicious Air*, won the Conference on Christianity and Literature's Book of the Year award in 2007. She was awarded a National Endowment for the Arts Literature Fellowship in 2011.

THE FRUIT OF THE SPIRIT

If the Spirit left me a bushel of pears
on the counter, I'd find it easier to believe
than any possession of peace

or self-control—waking without belly
dread or keeping Cherry Garcia
in the freezer for more than twelve hours.

And joy and gentleness? When my son
spills a lime green Megaslush in the car,
I should sing, *Let's call the paper towel fairy!*

but instead bang the dash: *Crap!*
Pay more attention! and tail the fluff-headed
Bonneville driver all the way home.

The fruit aren't commands, but signs,
I've been taught, evidence of genuine faith.
I thought I'd crucified this nonsense

with the flesh. Have you forsaken me,
Christ? Or have I never believed?
Come on, you didn't say shit, He says.

And the ice cream made it past
the ten-hour mark. That's as sweet
as peaches in August, my friend,

that's juice running down my beard.

THE ANGEL OVER PATMOS

Such a burden of beasts
and rainbows, sulfur and emeralds
leaking from his knapsack
as John hunches in a cave down there,
picking at a skeleton of fish.

The body resists exile.
Even the smallest burrowing mite
is enough to make John claw his skin,
saltwater stiffening his hair
like the driftwood he tries to burn.

Any sort of trance is impossible
to achieve when shifting on rocks,
the fabric of your robe sticking
in your crack. But with time,
the Spirit will come.

The angel doodles dragons
in the air. He circles like a plane on hold
and waits for the one twilight
John will sigh, lift his chapped hands,
and receive his words like wounds.

Brett Foster (1973–2015)

Born in Wichita, Kansas, Brett Foster earned a BA at the University of Missouri and a PhD at Yale and was a Wallace Stegner Fellow at Stanford University. The author of two books of poems, both published by Northwestern University Press, Foster was also a Renaissance scholar who edited or wrote four scholarly volumes on Shakespeare and his sources.

Packed with literary references in a conversational diction that is as natural musing on Plotinus as it is contemplating the pleasures of a sponge bath, Foster's poetry is governed by a loose meter and an intelligence that is both playful and intense. He has remarked that while poetry can be "a place to work out ideas," it is "more centrally" a place to work out "the heart's matters, the cries of the heart—those things that the mind would deign to ponder, or might be confounded by. . . . It's a place that is free, open, safe, and surprising." We see that "working out" of the heart's matters in the poems collected in this volume. In "The Garbage Eater," for example, Foster takes on the voice of a cult leader in California to explore our fear of death and rejection. In "At the City Church in San Francisco," Foster recounts his divided attention during a church service, distracted as he is by a beauty of a California morning in the background, "Golden Gate in the distance, those orange altars, / the bay beyond with its long, silver wings / and perfect bursts of plant life everywhere." Foster confesses his weakness before concluding the poem with a dazzling resolution.

Winner of the Willis Barnstone Prize for poetry translation in 2010 and the Baltimore Review Poetry Prize for his poem "On the Numbness That Will Be Our Future," Foster was also the recipient of grants from the PEN American Center and the Illinois Arts Council. He was a professor of English and Poet in Residence at Wheaton College in Illinois until 2015 when he died from cancer at the age of 42.

THE GARBAGE EATER

Fear of dying, fear of death:
those phobias came easy, shaped
nightly by a little boy's breath

talking out a clockwork afterlife
with parents till I fell asleep.
Most Sunday-school kids peddled
the Gospels or got lost in the deep
troughs of Apocalypse—the dead
rising, the Antichrist, the grief
or wonder, His Passion, a hundred
visions. They loved the thrill of belief;
for me, the impossible Law: I kept
reading Leviticus and felt the toll
of Numbers' rules. Eighteen and severe,
I learned to meditate on the soul's
needs. Like a desert hermit I read
Jerome's book and those Greek scrolls

of the Church Fathers, and the fear
of dying lessened, the fear of death
diminished by the Christocentric Rapture,

promise of its timeless kingdom, reign
of faithful infinitely singing there.
But unmoored grace is dangerous.
It must be guarded every hour
against the body's ignominious abuse,
the mindless evils of a worldly brain.
When I quit school, my parents made a fuss
about my teacher-leader, who explained
the stain of sin was like a gnawing whore
only killed by full attention.
I shaved my hair off, wore a wreath
to scar my forehead bloody. Under my chin
a beard hangs in a tangled mess. I'm homeless—
eat the world's crap, sleep in tarpaulin.

The physical means nothing beneath
the small fear of dying, which fears
only unworthiness more than death.

AT THE CITY CHURCH OF SAN FRANCISCO

Not a thousand tongues singing this morning,
but enough to fill up the little space,
Main Post Chapel of the Presidio,

lovely, if only temporary home
for the gathered, this young body of Christ,
new church which soon will need someplace bigger.

Attending with friends, themselves becoming
members this service, I want to follow
like one who has relinquished everything,

but struggle just to get the hymns right, or
understand the passage from Luke's gospel.
How to preach with so much that's beautiful

around us? Sunlight heating the sandstone,
red brick of the military buildings
stately and from another century,

Golden Gate in the distance, those orange altars,
the bay beyond with its long, silver wings
and perfect bursts of plant life everywhere—

I saw these things just walking from the car.
The pastor is a man of faith indeed,
attempting exegesis in the midst of this.

I try to resist as they go forward,
focus on the chancel rail they walk toward.
But as they raise their hands to take the pledge,

my eyes seize the motion just below
the sanctuary beams. Shadows of eucalyptus
or transplanted cypress pass over

a lone panel of stained glass like river
water across smooth, prismatic rock,
dimpling with light an androgynous saint,

animate, zealous for the cause, hungry
to cheer the tired ones, heal the invalids,
and the standing lead hobbling to the kingdom.

James Matthew Wilson (1975)

James Matthew Wilson's poetry is both confessional and classical. At ease writing about bikinied lifeguards or Odysseus's return home in meter and rhyme "that click into place," as he puts it in his introduction to *Some Permanent Things*, Wilson is thoroughly contemporary and thoroughly informed by the Western tradition. Sick of "the past / Being squashed flat by prosperity's hard thumb," he writes in "Verse Letter to Jason," Wilson attempts to reshape the present with the refracting forms of the past. In his foreword to *The Hanging God*, Dana Gioia observes that "Wilson writes in what one might call the high humanist Christian tradition. In literary terms, this is not the music of the humble shepherd's pipe but the double keyboard pipe organ—resonant, complex, and contrapuntal." His examples are Robert Lowell and Richard Wilbur, John Donne and George Herbert, as well as the later T. S. Eliot.

His overtly religious work draws from the Church calendar and religious rituals. He is the author of a series of poems on Advent and on the Stations of the Cross, as well as individual poems on holy days and Catholic saints. Included in this volume are "Passover," "After the Ascension," and "Some Will Remember You," a meditative poem on Edith Stein, Saint Teresa Benedicta of the Cross, a Jew and a nun in the Carmelite Order who died in Auschwitz in 1942. She was canonized in 1987.

Wilson was born in 1975. He was, until 2021, an associate professor of Humanities and Augustinian Traditions at Villanova. He is currently Professor of Humanities and the Founding Director of the Master of Fine Arts program in Creative Writing at the University of Saint Thomas in Houston. He is the author of several books, including *The Hanging God*, *The River of the Immaculate Conception*, and *The Strangeness of the Good*. He won the Hiett Prize in the Humanities from the Dallas Institute of Humanities and Culture in 2017 and has twice been awarded the Lionel Basney Award by the Conference for Christianity and Literature.

PASSOVER

A woman sitting in a restaurant,
Over a plate of rice and Chinese pork,
Holds back her hair with one hand, with the other
Presses flat the cheap paperback she's reading.
I see her there and think about those times
I've sat in hotel lounges with a beer
And waited for someone to ask about
The weather. But, it's early in the evening.
The bar staff's busy cutting fruit and stocking
Their knee-high fridges tight with jilting bottles.
They glance at me a couple times, as if
Confused that I'd disrupt their busy quiet.
Before real customers drown out the muzak.

  A few years back, my chimney started smoking.
This was just after Christmas, or, now that
I think about it, maybe just before.
I called a sweep, and from the second he
Got his black sheets spread round the hearth and set
His tools up in an expert semicircle,
He never once—not once, I'm sure—stopped talking.

  At first, he wanted to describe the workings
Of damper, heat shield, chimney: to extol
The virtues of some mason long ago
Who could not hear us but had done good work.
And then, by turns, he started talking of
The miracles of the Old Testament,
The cross-shaped splattering of blood the Jews
In Egypt brushed upon their doors, one night,
To signal that the angels bringing death
Should pass them by. I saw the other children
Lying in their cribs with fingers curled toward heaven
Or what had snatched their breath. Was he a scout
Or something from some tin shack Bible Church,
Set where the hills go flat, where split-railed horse farms
Give way to sodden fields and trailer parks?

He was, or had been, so he said, at last,
A junior champ in some state scripture quiz.
I signed a check and showed him to the door.
  We wait and wait, as if it were a kind of digging
Through ashes for a buried, burning ember.
We press the spines of books until they crack,
And when we've seen their stories to the end,
We do not know what we're to do with them,
As if they're strangers stopped at the wrong house.

SOME WILL REMEMBER YOU

The work of salvation takes place in obscurity and stillness. In the heart's quiet dialogue with God the living building blocks out of which the kingdom of God grows are prepared, the chosen instruments for the construction forged.
  —St. Teresa Benedicta of the Cross

I

Some will remember you for what they call you,
A curious fact or novelty, and some will
Remember chiefly how you died, and linger
On blood's enthralling stain. Still others may
Enter within that final silence, find
The life that did not know it begged salvation,
But the mere clarity of things and thought;
The one who chattered in the corridors
Of being, took tea with Husserl, before
The interior mountain beckoned you to climb,
The floors of the self-darkened room first creaked.
You wrote out what you saw and then sought stillness.
And not for what you said but what you were,
Not for your truest name, you were packed off
To death. After the smoke, bones left forgotten,
Your jotted notes shut in a metal trunk,
As others bore reprisals and arrests,
Your thought lived in the study of a priest.

II

In evil times and aftertimes, in times
When all the stubbled fields of action smolder,
Bowed heads can't help but make their patient study
Of how the person worlds. In his wired room—
With worship driven back through unmarked doors,
And the earth gutted by the tread of foreign
Tanks—he would read your half-lost books, would speak
Their words into the empty air for all
The stashed and sensitive microphones to hear.
In those times, your words, carried on the quiet,
Fostered his own. Thought, act, and judging person,
The self in solitude revealing God.
Clicked like the murdered signal of your voice
Across a telegraph and moved his hand.
Below the frequencies of State radio,
That remnant bookish beauty leaned into
His ear: a ghostly Carmelite with time
Enough to stipple out accented thoughts,
On where our thinking natures drive themselves.

While you were still a student, restless, hard,
Unchained still from the science of the cross,
Too lost in thought to think a knock could come,
The brown shirts there to haul your body off
Beyond its cloistral habit, even then
Your tattered typescripts sealed within themselves
A whole new vision of our thinking, living,
Our radiant way of knowing through our seeing.
And these, in time, would fill Wojtyla's head,
Though you'd have long mixed ashes with the dead.

III

What terrible love did she bear
The soldiers massed about the steeple,
Breaking the sisters from their prayer?
"Come, we are going for our people."

Pressed in the rattling cattle car
Between her sister and rough board,
Drawn through the final smoke of war?
"Come, we are going to our Lord."

IV

This life: she'd graphed its pattern on the page,
The frail inconstant forms of bone and speech,
And gave to one mind, tranquil in an age
Of violence, wisdom which no war could reach.
Not in her name as Jew or Carmelite;
Not just in death, her study's parasite;
But in the working out of truth and choice,
In words that prayed when others lapsed to rage,
She'd guide, perhaps, the bullet, guide the voice
Of John Paul up the mountain of an age.

V

Those years after,
The Successor
From his throne,
Voice hoarse, intoned
That she was neither
Casualty nor teacher,
But philosopher,
And holy martyr,
Jewish daughter,
Church's doctor,
Spiritual mother,
Illumined voice
Of reason and choice,
A converted heart
Who'd played her part,
A sainted sign
Named Edith Stein.

Shane McCrae (1975)

Shane McRae, born in Portland, Oregon, in 1975, serves as poetry editor at *Image* and is the author of seven books of poetry. He has received the Whiting Award, the Lannon Literary Award, a National Endowment for the Arts Fellowship and a Guggenheim Fellowship, among other honors. Having dropped out of high school and subsequently earned a GED, McRae holds both an MFA in poetry from the University of Iowa Writers' Workshop and a Juris Doctorate from Harvard University.

Details of McRae's childhood, raw and vivid, have been laid bare in his poetry. The son of a white mother and a black father, he was kidnapped at age three by his mother's parents and reared in an abusive, white-supremacist household. An after-school television special about suicide introduced him, in a life-transforming encounter, to the poems of Sylvia Plath. In a figure for the way that both poetic and religious tradition operate for him, McRae reflects, in a 2016 interview with Cate Lycurgus of *32 Poems*, on a triggering idea behind his collection, *Animals Too Big to Kill*:

> I was thinking . . . about what an animal made of all the animals I've ever eaten would look like, since traces, or traces of traces, of those animals are inside of and also constitute my body. The animal would certainly be much larger than I am, and I imagine larger than any animal that has ever lived, and I carry its ghost and possibility with me.

Implicit in this imagery is the idea of something which has died—the ghost, the consumed animal—but at the same time lives forward, though broken down from its original form, filling subsequent lives, filled always with "possibility." The image suggests a particularly Christian way to understand questions of identity and trauma through art: to find ways to put to death the sins of the past, in such a way that they are not forgotten but remade. For a poet like McRae, the act of writing may become an act of forgiveness—an act which makes things new, without erasing the marks of the nails.

This act speaks also to a dynamic relationship with the poetic tradition which has formed him. McRae has spoken, in his *Harvard* magazine interview, of his intense connection with English Renaissance poetry: "I had this rule that I would not do anything metrically that Sir Philip Sidney would not have recognized as valid." Though the contemporary reader might not readily intuit the English Renaissance in McRae's visceral, fractured lines, still the contemporary work asserts, "I carry its ghost and possibility with me."

LORD OF THE HOPELESS ALSO DEAR

Lord of the hopeless also dear   Hat-Soak

Pole-in-the-Canal and Red-Tie Father   Son

And Holy Ghost not   in that order break

The rottenness of those who torture one

Of Thy least wrath-deserving exiles me

Not   wholly undeserving   no   but some

And isn't it the some that counts with Thee

O   Gondola also as the trees pass warm

Overhead I   can close my eyes and they

Are almost not   burning and this is any

River to the sea O   Lord I do not say

Release me call me home forgive my many

Sins I say Lord forgive my torturers

Who hate my faults   as if my faults were theirs

STILL WHEN I PICTURE IT THE FACE OF GOD IS A WHITE MAN'S FACE

Before it disappears

on the sand his long white   beard before it disappears

The face of the man

in the waves I ask her does she see it ask her does

The old man in the waves   as the waves crest she see it does

she see the old man his

White   his face crumbling face it looks

as old as he's as old as

The ocean looks

and for a moment almost looks

His face like it's   all the way him

As never such old skin

looks my / Daughter age four

She thinks it might he might be real she shouts *Hello*

And after there's no answer answers *No*

Benjamin Myers (1975)

Benjamin Myers writes in a variety of modes. On the one hand, we find lyrical descriptions of the natural world that show the same attention to detail and drama as Jane Kenyon and Robert Frost, as in "Field," which is included in this volume. On the other hand, his poems, particularly in his latest collection, *Black Sunday*, are marked by a narrative turn to the past. Set during the Dust Bowl of the 1930s, Myers speaks in the voice of various characters—a farmer, his wife, their daughter, the town minister, the town drunk, and others. In an interview for *World Literature Today*, Myers remarked that "While I admire poets like Frank O'Hara who can be totally in the moment, my poems are often an attempt to inhabit the past and the present simultaneously."

If his poems attempt to "inhabit the past and the present simultaneously," they also attempt to inhabit this and the other world simultaneously. Again, "Field" is a good example—it is a dream of heaven but as a specific moment in the past that is rendered present by sensuous detail ("my granddad's '72 Ford, still smelling / of oilfield and aftershave"). Myer's work also presents us with a sharp critique of the sentimentality that can be a problem for Christian artists, as he wrote in his essay "The Sentimentality Trap."

Myers is currently the Crouch-Mathis Professor of Literature at Oklahoma Baptist University. The author of three volumes of poetry, including *Elegy for Trains*, which won the 2011 Oklahoma Book Award for Poetry, Myers was the Poet Laureate of Oklahoma from 2015 to 2016. His poems have appeared in *The Yale Review, Image, 32 Poems, The Christian Century*, and many other journals. He received a BA in English from the University of the Ozarks and a PhD from Washington University in St. Louis.

THE REVEREND ON NATURAL THEOLOGY

Seeing God in nature do
you see Him crucified? The rabbit ripped
by dogs, its guts strewn across a crew-
cut field, the hide left wet where it was stripped?
Driving through countryside you sometimes see
a line of coyote pelts hung from barbed fence,
flapped by high wind, bothered with flies and flea
infested, bullet holes in all the skins.
Do you then read the Book of Nature's red
ink dribbled down the posts? Consider all
the world's wide gore, the white-tailed deer that's spread
across the road, the earth's unlapped offal.
Everything broken must be broken again.
I will make you fissures of men.

FIELD

Heaven is a field I am
driving an old truck across
in the only dream I have
on the subject. The sky over
that pasture is so blue I know
it will burst if it doesn't turn
twenty different reds
at evening. The truck
is my granddad's '72 Ford, still smelling
of oilfield and aftershave. When it stalls
I get out and lift the hood but look
instead into the everlasting distance
dotted with cattle and streaked
with blotches where the henbit
has bruised the pasture purple.
I think of my father lifting
me onto his lap to let
me drive as we bumped over clumps

of gopher dirt in the pasture,
how I steered
wildly through the grass
his boot barely on the gas.
But it is my father-
in-law who is standing
next to me when I look,
who has bloodied his knuckles
starting the engine
running again, who is gesturing
with a patience he rarely had
in life for me to get back
into the truck and drive on.

I wake to hear our children breathe their sleep
one room over, and to tell you, love
of all my lifetime, as we lie beneath
our ceiling in the middle
of our bed, that heaven
has a field full
of fathers. I have been
there. I am one of them.

Mark Wagenaar (1979)

Mark Wagenaar is the author of two poetry collections: a 2012 debut, *The Body Distances*, and *Southern Tongues Leave Us Shining*, winner of the 2016 Benjamin Saltman Poetry Award and published by Red Hen Press in 2018. He holds degrees from the University of Northern Iowa, the University of Virginia, and the University of North Texas. In addition to the Benjamin Saltman Award, his honors include the Auburn Poetry of Witness Prize, the Oberon Poetry Prize, the *New Letters* Poetry Prize, the *Poetry International* Prize, and many others.

Like the contemporary American poet Charles Wright, often cited as an influence, Wagenaar invests himself imaginatively in a universe in which an intangible and elusive sense of mystery permeates every physical detail. For Wagenaar this mystery is an explicitly Christian one, grounded in the scriptural narrative of salvation. In his poems, that narrative reiterates itself through an associative unrolling of images in which notions of death and life, sin and grace, present themselves in striking and unexpected guises, as unlikely visions in which something more real than their own reality makes itself present. If deer are "apparitional," direct revelations of the divine reality, goats on the other hand—devouring scavengers, uncouth in their ugly physicality—still, in "salvag[ing]" random debris, carrying it in their bodies so that it is "rescued from time's indignities," become figures for mercy. Though their coming and going enacts its own kind of apparition, it is an apparition of a grace mediated through fallenness, as fallen human beings can apprehend it. This, ultimately, is the "Goat Hour Gospel," the unlikely good news of the goat. The biblical Abel, meanwhile, "Almost Asleep in the Field," between the Fall and his realization of that Fall in the fact of his own death, finds himself caught in a tension in which the aliveness of the world presses itself upon him—bagworms spinning, the skin of a peach breaking—even in its processes of destruction and decay. As he waits for sleep to take him, he is paradoxically awake to what he does not know: "that gravity bends light." Like the world around him, but with the capacity for understanding which the rest of the created order lacks, he feels in his own aliveness, in his awareness of the coming night, the approach of the mystery of death, the shadow—his own—which he cannot see.

Goat Hour Gospel (Such Salvage)

Just as the evening's about to move on, they appear, not as the
  apparitional deer—
here, & gone in the next moment, without a sound—but one by one,

bumbling through briar, chewing through poison ivy, sniffing at trees.
A slow procession walking beneath elms & birches that hold up the last
  light.

And you're alone with the traces of things, the news in front of you:
the crooked skeleton of Richard III was dug up from a parking lot,

humpbacked, once buried in his boots & battlefield wounds. Nearby a
  lost river
has been uncovered, & coughed up its mouthful of Roman skulls.

No relic is safe, it seems, from an invisible tide that presses them upward.
Sometimes it's not the loss that hurts but the indignities of the discovery.

And yet beside the diggers & builders of new things is this mangy
  congregation,
pushing through the scrub without a trail or blueprint or direction.

Their dirty white fur shines a little in this late, lost hour.
They bleat as they shamble & piss on each other without warning,

or maybe as a warning, or in greeting. They'll eat anything—tin can,
T-shirt, canvas sack, bones of animals & kings, & carry them awhile.

And so do we: each night, across the country, people turn up at hospitals
unable to speak, for the needle or nail lodged

in their throats. They're unable to explain why, but we know—
that desperate mix of need & panic that can drive us to keep something
  safe

for good. These dearest items take your words & leave them luminous,
radiolucent, shining on the X-ray, like this swallowed ring: a ghostly
 eclipse.

Small comfort to share an appetite with these goats, this dishevelled lot.
But a comfort, too, to know that some things will be saved from the soil,

rescued from time's indignities, if only for a little while, & by these
 scruffy
reliquaries, on the other side of the valley now, flickering slightly

as they near the vanishing point of the timberline. And we might call
such salvage *mercy*. And it must be even for the undeserving,

for those of us who didn't live right, or live best. Whatever that means.
Mercy will find us, even when we fail to recognize it, when we least
 expect it.

Abel, Almost Asleep in the Field

When I'm still
I hear the bagworms twist in their cities of clouds
in the elms & maples.
I hear something break the skin on one of the peaches
in the branches above me, almost

I can hear the light strike their fuzzy globes

(What becomes of the four pounds of sunlight that strikes the earth
each second? One day someone will discover
                                    what we are born knowing,

that gravity bends light
& just as the earth draws the light
so does each body

pull us, our five-, seven-, ten stone enough
to pull someone,

even a trace
a hairstrand a shadow),

a sound as quiet as someone wandering without direction,
half of him in sun, just like the earth.

Filling his pockets with stones. And even quieter
than a long look at a river

are death's two hundred horses, mouthing the dark without a sound,
as quiet as forgiveness.

Their hooves resound in me like the steps of every one I have called brother.

A horizon as dark as horses,

as crows descending, a distance

dark as the throat of God. The shadow I cast
                                    I cannot see.

Ryan Wilson (1982)

Ryan Wilson's collection of poems, *The Stranger World*, which was awarded the Donald Justice Poetry Prize in 2017, is full of doubleness. The voice is Wilson's, but never does he speak to us directly. He speaks, rather, through translation, in the voices of Baudelaire or Horace, or through personas—a man at a party, a modern Samaritan, a husband plagued by a domestic mystery. These voices are frequently alienated from themselves and others. In "Man at the Party," for example, which draws from the language of T. S. Eliot's "Hollow Men," Wilson writes:

> We are the men of inattentive shrugs
> And accident, of oops and beg your pardon
> Nosing through vacuity like slugs
> At home in winter's disremembered garden . . .

Wilson's preferred stanza is an ABAB quatrain, but the self-similarity of form only heightens the sense of uncanniness that Wilson's poems create. We recognize the world of *The Stranger World* and ourselves in the speakers, but the world is also not ours, the speakers not us, and we, it slowly becomes apparent, not who we think we are. "We do not dream," Wilson writes in "The Pest," "We toss like unknown planets in a void. / Inhabited silences edge us toward a scream. / We grasp each other, wild to be destroyed."

What is the lesson here, if there is a lesson? "You cannot change your life," Wilson writes in "In the Harvest Season," which is collected below: "Give up; give thanks." This is Wilson's response to Rainer Marie Rilke, who writes famously in "Archaic Torso of Apollo" that "You must change your life." For Wilson, this is a half-truth. You must, yes, but cannot change your life.

Wilson earned a BA from the University of Georgia, an MFA from Johns Hopkins University, and a second MFA from Boston University. He is the editor-in-chief of *Literary Matters*, the online publication of the Association of Literary Scholars, Critics, and Writers, and has been awarded, among other prizes, the Sankey Prize for Excellence in Poetry by Johns Hopkins University and the Shmuel Traum Prize by Boston University. His poems have appeared in *The Sewanee Review*, *The Yale Review*, *The New Criterion*, *32 Poems*, and many other publications. His work was included in the 2018 edition of *Best American Poetry*.

XENIA

One day a silent man arrives
At your door in an outdated suit,
Threadbare and black, like a lost mourner
Or a Bible salesman who's been robbed.
Penniless, he needs a place to stay.
And you, magnanimous you, soon find
This stranger reading in your chair,
Eating your cereal, drinking your tea,
Or standing in your clothes at the window
Awash in afternoon's alien light.

You tire of his constant company.
Your floorboards creak with his shuffling footfalls,
Haunting dark rooms deep in the night.
You lie awake in blackness, listening,
Cursing the charity or pride
That opened up the door for him
And wonder how to explain yourself.
He smells like durian and smoke
But it's mostly his presence, irksome, fogging
The mind up like breath on a mirror . . .

You practice cruelty in a mirror,
Then practice sympathetic faces.
You ghoul. Your cunning can't deceive you.
You are afraid to call your friends
For help, knowing what they would say.
It's just you two. You throw a fit when
He sneaks water into the whisky bottle,
Then make amends. You have no choice
Except to learn humility,
To love this stranger as yourself,

Who won't love you, or ever leave.

In the Harvest Season

It's finished. Waiting's all that will remain.
The gossip now must go unverified.
Blue smoke from leaf-piles, smoldering like pride,
Hangs here, a ghost, a storm-cloud that can't rain.
Last night, the country's final weathervane
Fell in the high winds. Old roofs, stripped bare, preside.
Take down the ragged self you've crucified
And let the crows wing through the fields of grain.

The sagging fence will never stand up straight.
Whatever's not ripe now will never be.
The pain tormenting you will not abate,
And in the windows of vacated banks
You'll see yourself, passing by aimlessly.
You cannot change your life. Give up; give thanks.

Chelsea Wagenaar (1989)

Chelsea Wagenaar, who holds degrees from the University of Virginia and the University of North Texas, is the author of two books of poetry: *Mercy Spurs the Bone,* winner of the 2013 Philip Levine Prize in Poetry, and *The Spinning Place,* which received the 2018 Michael Waters Poetry Prize. In Wagenaar's poems, intimacies of marriage, childbearing, travel, and observation are set against a large vision which, as the title poem of her 2019 collection *The Spinning Place* suggest, encompasses the sweeping gestures of time: "Buildings rise and fall. Great crowds cross / borders. Capitals change names. Call of birds // gone extinct." The body's seasons of health and sickness, belonging and exile, integrate with both the turn of the physical universe and the time-outside-time of the Christian calendar. In this way she locates human experience in its larger context, the entire created order.

Her poem "Advent," for example, marries intimate human suffering—husband's slipped disc—to the more usual conflation of pregnancy's waiting with the liturgical season of Advent. The physical season, with its intimations of death, echoes the dimensions of the speaker's identification with the Virgin Mary, anticipating both joy and sorrow. As she seeks to alleviate the pain of one body's disintegration, another body builds itself inside her. Another pregnancy poem, "Scale," juxtaposes gestation not with Advent but Lent and its sense of journeying. The Lenten pilgrim, like the expectant mother, journeys in time, not space, "measure[d] / . . . in months, in so many weeks," though the body itself is also its own landscape, traveled through. It finds its echoes in contrails, in the swelling moon, in the "solstice" equilibrium of darkness and light.

In these poems, the human body appears as part of the body of the physical universe, made of matter, space, and time, but defined explicitly as the Body of Christ by its identification with liturgical time. These poems expand Paul's assertion in 1 Corinthians 12: "If one member suffers, all the members suffer with it." The very creation which, as Paul says elsewhere, groans in its birth pangs, both figures and is figured by the woman awaiting the birth of her child. The largeness of this vision, seeing through to the unity of all that God has made and "holds together in himself," exalts human experience not as something merely personal and private, but as an essential expression of and participation in that great unity.

ADVENT

Last week a jellied disc
in one of my husband's lower vertebrae
cinched, slipped—on the x-ray
the bones' thorned edges gritted against each other,
his whole spine yearning left,
a lily stem arched toward the promise
of light. Now the days shrink
into themselves, the trees bare-limbed
but for squirrels' nests and the green
bloom of mistletoe, the opalescent berries
suspended like droplets of milk.
All my comforts are questions:
is it better, does this help, and to wonder
at the body as host, his to pain,
mine to our firstborn. Unseen, unfelt
arms and legs push into socket,
joints form, the elbow a door
swinging open. Before you, before your
cloistral assembly of parts, I knew
words waiting to become you:
Face. Hair. Cuticle. Was it this way
for Mary, overshadowed by the Spirit?—
her body not hers, reworded with the promise
of flesh? *How can this be?* I echo her,
though I have known a man.
Here? I ask him, and soothe cream
into his skin, the two divots in the small
of his back—gates that keep the invisible hurt.
May it be as you have said—
and I picture her trembling hands,
the hour dusk, everything vague and blued,
hour all the shadows become shadow.

SCALE

> *I am soft sift*
> *In an hourglass*
> *—Hopkins*

Against the darkening winterplum sky,
a lone contrail whitens—loose thread, untufted
cotton. A perfect inverse of me:

                                        Lenten moon

of my belly taut, halved by a slurred gray line.
Linea nigra, the doctor says, my belly button's
new ashen tail a ghostly likeness of the cut cord

that once bound me to my mother.
These days I am a solstice, a season begun
in your germinal dark. Measure me now

in months, in so many weeks, all the streams
of my body downrivering
into the estuary that is you.

                                        That is you—

there, the tick of your limbs, a second hand,
a second hand, fingers whorled and filling
with bone, numbered one by one,

as are your days in that luminous book.
Nameless one, I know you in numbers.
Your parts, your gathering weeks, the 145

of your heart. The thrum of kicks
in an hour is as many as the sparrows
that flit in the bare snarl of vine and hedge,

as many as the houses that line our street,
my trips to the bathroom in the night.
I think, in those small, bleary hours,

of the hand that pens the book of our days,
turns the page. Nameless one, only once more
will you be numberless, when you begin again

at zero. Day you quicken toward, cold sear
of light, fugue of voices. You'll be cut
like yarn from the skein, your skin unshined

of blood, your heels grasped and slapped.
Cry, numberless one—for now you are laid
upon the scale, the 0.0 you'll shatter,

your life weighed against a feather,

                                    already counted up.

ACKNOWLEDGMENTS

We would like to thank the editorial staff at Paraclete Press—particularly Lillian Miao and Robert Edmonson—for their direction and support throughout the process of bringing this book to press. Thanks go to Dana Gioia, too, for his early and sustained encouragement, to Jessica Schnepp for her expert content editing, and to Margot Enns for her help with permissions. We are grateful to the poets and presses for permission to reprint the following poems:

William Baer, "Adam" from *Borges and Other Sonnets*. Copyright ©
    2003 by William Baer. Reprinted with the permission of the poet.
    "Snake," "Theotokos," and "Ethiopian" from *Psalter: A Sequence of
    Catholic Sonnets*. Copyright © 2011 by William Baer. Reprinted with
    permission.

Bruce Beasley, "All Saints" from *Theophobia*. Copyright © 2012 by Bruce
    Beasley. Reprinted with the permission of The Permissions Company,
    LLC, on behalf of BOA Editions, Ltd., www.boaeditions.org. "After
    an Adoration," "Consolation," and "Doxology" from *The Creation*.
    Copyright © 1994 by Bruce Beasley. Reprinted with permission.

Maryann Corbett, "State Fair Fireworks, Labor Day" from *Street View*.
    Copyright © 2017 Maryann Corbet. Used by permission of Able Muse
    Press. "Holiday Concert" from *Credo for the Checkout Line*. Copyright
    © 2013 Maryann Corbet. Used by permission of Able Muse Press.

Scott Cairns, "The More Earnest Prayer of Christ," "Possible Answers to
    Prayer," "Bad Theology: A Quiz," "Idiot Psalm 2," "Idiot Psalm 4," and
    "Dawn at Saint Anna's Skete" from *Slow Pilgrim: The Collected Poems*.
    Copyright © 2006, 2014, 2015 by Scott Cairns. Used by permission of
    Paraclete Press.

Brett Foster, "The Garbage Eater" and "At the City Church of San
    Francisco" from *The Garbage Eater*. Copyright © 2011 by Brett Foster.
    Published 2011 by TriQuarterly Books/Northwestern University Press.
    All rights reserved.

Benjamin Myers, "The Reverend on Natural Theology" from *Black Sunday*. Copyright © 2019 by Benjamin Myers. "Field" first appeared in *Image Journal*, number 90. Reprinted with permission.

Marilyn Nelson, "Churchgoing" from *For the Body*, "Incomplete Renunciation" from *Magnificat*, and "For the Feast of Corpus Christi" from *Faster than Light*. Copyright © 1978, 1994, 2012 by Marilyn Nelson. Used by permission of Louisiana State University Press. "Miracle in the Collection Plate" from *My Seneca Village*. Copyright © 2015 by Marilyn Nelson. Used by permission of namelos, llc. "The Temperance Flu" from *Meeting House*. Copyright © 2015 by Marilyn Nelson. Reprinted with permission.

Kathleen Norris, "Prayer to Eve," "Little Girls in Church," "The Sky Is Full of Blue, and Full of the Mind of God," and "Ascension" from *Journey: New and Selected Poems 1969-1999*. Copyright © 2001 by Kathleen Norris. Reprinted by permission of the University of Pittsburgh Press.

Angela Alaimo O'Donnell, "To Be a Pilgrim" from *Still Pilgrim* and "Flannery's Manifesto" from *Andalusian Hours*. Copyright © 2017 and 2020 by Angela Alaimo O'Donnell. Reprinted by permission of Paraclete Press.

Jay Parini, "At the Ruined Monastery of Amalfi" from *Town Life*. Copyright © 1988 by Jay Parini. Reprinted by permission of Henry Holt and Company. All Rights Reserved. Electronic version reprinted by the permission of the Elaine Markson Literary Agency. "Blessings" and "Grammar of Affection" from *New and Collected Poems: 1975-2015*. Copyright © 2016 by Jay Parini. Reprinted by permission of Beacon Press, Boston.

John Poch, "Ignored Woodwork in Old Churches" from *Fix Quiet*. Copyright © 2016 by John Poch. Used by permission of St. Augustine's Press.

Jennifer Reeser, "Nature Does Not Care" and "O Great Spirit" from *Indigenous*. Copyright © 2019 by Jennifer Reeser. Used by permission of Able Muse Press.

Clare Rossini, "Fra Angelico's 'Annunciation' at San Marco" from *Winter Morning with Crow*. Copyright © 1997 by Clare Rossini. Reprinted by permission of the University of Akron Press. Unauthorized duplication not permitted. "Prayer of Sorts" from *Lingo*. Copyright © 2006 by Clare Rossini. Reprinted by permission of the University of Akron Press. Unauthorized duplication not permitted.

Tania Runyan, "The Fruit of the Spirit" from *Second Sky*. Copyright © 2013 by Tania Runyan. Used by permission of Wipf and Stock Publishers, www.wipfandstock.com. "The Angel Over Patmos" from *What Will Soon Take Place*. Copyright © 2017 by Tania Runyan. Reprinted by permission of Paraclete Press.

Robert B. Shaw, "Things We Will Never Know" and "Ash Wednesday, Late Afternoon" from *Wonder of Seeing Double*. Copyright © 1988 by Robert B. Shaw. Reprinted by permission of the University of Massachusetts University Press. "A Geode" from *Below the Surface*. Copyright © 1999 by Robert B. Shaw. Reprinted by permission. "Dec. 23" and "Pilgrims" from *Solving for X*. Copyright © 2002 by Robert B. Shaw. Reprinted with the permission of Ohio University Press.

Tracy K. Smith, "Cathedral Kitsch," "My God, It's Full of Stars," and "The Universe as Primal Scream" from *Life on Mars*. Copyright © 2011 by Tracy K. Smith. "Wade in the Water" and "The Garden of Eden" from *Wade in the Water*. Copyright © 2018 by Tracy K. Smith. All reprinted with the permission of The Permissions Company, LLC on behalf of Graywolf Press, Minneapolis, MN, www.graywolfpress.org.

Mark Wagenaar, "Goat Hour Gospel" and "Abel, Almost Asleep in the Field" from *Southern Tongues Leave Us Shining*. Copyright © 2018 by Mark Wagenaar. Reprinted by permission for Red Hen Press.

Chelsea Wagenaar, "Advent" and "Scale" from The Spinning Place. Copyright © 2019 by Chelsea Wagenaar. Reprinted by permission of Southern Indiana Review Press.

INDEX OF TITLES

THE EDITORS

Micah Mattix is the poetry editor at *First Things* and an associate professor of English at Regent University. His criticism has appeared in *The Wall Street Journal*, *The Atlantic*, *The New Criterion*, *National Review*, *Humanities*, and many other outlets. Previously he was the literary editor at *The American Conservative* and a contributing editor to *The Weekly Standard*. He is currently a senior editor at *Spectator World* and the author of *The Soul Is a Stranger in this World: Essays on Poets and Poetry*.

Sally Thomas is the author of a poetry collection, *Motherland*, a finalist for the 2018 Able Muse Book Award and published by Able Muse Press in 2020. She is also the author of a novel, *Works of Mercy*, published by Wiseblood Books in 2022. Over the last three decades, her poetry, fiction, reviews, and essays have appeared in such journals as *First Things*, *Plough Quarterly*, *Public Discourse*, and the *New Yorker*. She serves as Associate Poetry Editor for the *New York Sun*.

IRON PEN

O that my words were written down!
O that they were inscribed in a book!
O that with an iron pen and with lead
they were engraved on a rock forever!
—Job 19:23–24

Outcast and utterly alone, Job pours out his anguish to his Maker. From the depths of his pain, he reveals a trust in God's goodness that is stronger than his despair, giving humanity some of the most beautiful and poetic verses of all time. Paraclete's Iron Pen imprint is inspired by this spirit of unvarnished honesty and tenacious hope.

OTHER IRON PEN BOOKS

Almost Entirely, Jennifer Wallace, 2017
Andalusian Hours, Angela Alaimo O'Donnell, 2020
Angels Everywhere, Luci Shaw, 2022
Begin with a Question, Marjorie Maddox, 2022
The Consequence of Moonlight, Sofia Starnes, 2018
Cornered by the Dark, Harold J. Recinos, 2021
Eye of the Beholder, Luci Shaw, 2018
Exploring This Terrain, Margaret B. Ingraham, 2020
From Shade to Shine, Jill Peláez Baumgaertner, 2022
The Generosity, Luci Shaw, 2020
Glory in the Margins, Nikki Grimes, 2021
Idiot Psalms, Scott Cairns, 2014
Iona, Kenneth Steven, 2021
Litany of Flights, Laura Reece Hogan, 2020
Raising the Sparks, Jennifer Wallace, 2022
Still Pilgrim, Angela Alaimo O'Donnell, 2017
There Is a Future, Amy Bornman, 2020
Thérèse, Sarah Law, 2020
To Shatter Glass, Sister Sharon Hunter, CJ, 2021
Wing Over Wing, Julie Cadwallader Staub, 2019

ABOUT PARACLETE PRESS

PARACLETE PRESS is the publishing arm of the Cape Cod Benedictine community, the Community of Jesus. Presenting a full expression of Christian belief and practice, we reflect the ecumenical charism of the Community and its dedication to sacred music, the fine arts, and the written word.

SCAN
TO
READ
MORE

Learn more about us at our website:
www.paracletepress.com
or phone us toll-free at 1.800.451.5006